I0892819

Rave Reviews

Rave Reviews

The History of Tuesday Musical

General Editor
Thomas Bacher

Contributing Editors
Sharon Cebula &
Cynthia L. Harrison

Ringtaw Books
Akron, Ohio

Copyright © 2014 by The University of Akron Press
All rights reserved • First Edition 2014 • Manufactured in the United States of America. All inquiries and permission requests should be addressed to the Publisher, The University of Akron Press, Akron, Ohio 44325–1703.

17 16 15 14 13 5 4 3 2 1

ISBN: 978-1-931968-95-9 (CLOTH)
ISBN: 978-1-937378-53-0 (PAPER)

LIBRARY OF CONGRESS CONTROL NUMBER: 2012947642

∞ The paper used in this publication meets the minimum requirements of ANSI / NISO Z39.48–1992 (Permanence of Paper).

Cover: Photograph of Renée Fleming by Andrew Eccles, used with permission; photograph of Yo-Yo Ma by Todd Rosenberg, used with permission; photograph of early members of Tuesday Musical from the Tuesday Musical Collection, University of Akron Archives. Design by Triad Communications.

All images and illustrations appearing in the book are courtesy of Tuesday Musical Association, unless otherwise noted.

Rave Reviews was designed and typeset in Stone Print by Amy Freels, with the assistance of Lauren McAndrews, and printed on sixty-pound natural and bound by Bookmasters of Ashland, Ohio.

Contents

Foreword

As a music critic covering Tuesday Musical for nearly two decades, I came to know and depend on an organization that has carved out a deservedly special place in the Akron community and the music world at large. Listeners can count on Tuesday Musical to present top-ranked talents, reaching and challenging the high bar set over the years by guests like Jascha Heifetz, Vladimir Horowitz, Luciano Pavarotti, and Renée Fleming. Tuesday Musical doesn't just follow; it also leads, identifying and nurturing the next generation of talent by bringing in guests like Joshua Bell early in his career. (It's telling that this group had the stature and reputation to attract Joshua Bell back *after* he became one of the world's most acclaimed violinists.)

Tuesday Musical has weathered societal changes, choosing to evolve without losing its identity. Once upon a time, Tuesday Musical Club was an all-volunteer group run by musically-trained women who did not work outside the home. In more recent years, Tuesday Musical Association's membership rolls have included both men and women. Monthly meetings welcome enthusiasts who do not have advanced musical training, yet they still offer the musicians among them the option of performing for each other—just for the joy of it.

A paid staff continues the tradition of a concert hall series, while an intimate, innovative *FUZE!* series, held in collaboration with the Akron Art Museum, branched out to introduce listeners to new sounds. Tuesday Musical feeds the spirit of loyal longtime listeners while extending a friendly hand to the next generation. Through substantial and personable in-school workshops, as well as through an impressively extensive voucher program that provides students with free tickets, Tuesday Musical has connected young people directly to the classical music tradition and laid the groundwork for the next generations of listeners.

It was one of Tuesday Musical's most ardent and creative supporters, pianist Margaret Baxtresser, who invited me to her home to meet representatives of Akron's arts organizations when I first moved here from Chicago. I quickly discovered the determined "quest for the best" that existed at Tuesday Musical. And if you attend a concert today, you can see the pleasure on the faces of performers when they sing or play for this organization's audience, which is surely one of the most well-educated, open, and responsive collection of listeners to be found. Where else but in Akron could such an extraordinary group as Tuesday Musical exist?

Long may you thrive.

Elaine Guregian
Former music critic, *Akron Beacon Journal*

Editor's Note

The compilation of this volume took more than a year, and although every effort was made to ensure the reliability of the information, it is possible some inconsistencies might be found. The story of Tuesday Musical was researched and verified using countless sources. Many individuals dug through various archives, genealogy records, newspaper stories, and other related documents to provide a thorough history of one of Akron's gems—an organization that has brought world-class performers to the area for over a century.

While it is difficult to thank everyone involved with the project, two individuals made substantial contributions: Sharon Cebula and Cynthia L. Harrison. Without their dedicated work, the pictorial history section would not be as rich as it is. The amount of information they uncovered is remarkable and adds depth to the story.

At the Press, Amy Freels, as well as Carol Slatter, were instrumental in completion of this project. In many ways, the story of Tuesday Musical became a story of people picking up certain tasks and finding out the answers. Then again, the story itself was compelling and many individual threads needed to be followed to give the story the breadth it deserved. We hope the story reflects the vibrant nature of the Tuesday Musical Association.

Acknowledgements

There are so many individuals who were pivotal in the telling of this story, but one name sums up all the parts and pieces of this project: Marcianne Herr. As a Tuesday Musical member and past president, Marcianne was the lady whose vision and persistent efforts guided this journey.

Marcianne was aided by other Tuesday Musical members who served on her archives committee: Harriet Boggs, Anna Mae Cummings, Laurie Gilles, Carolyn Durway, David Kellogg, and Corrinne Rohrbacher. Dale Dong put many hours of research into the photographs.

Tuesday Musical must also thank Cynthia Knight, in whose honor the Patron Award was established in 2007. Recipients of this award are recognized for their generous and continuous patronage of Tuesday Musical and others who have received this award include Dr. Kenneth F. Swanson, Donald and Corrinne Rohrbacher, and the anonymous donor of the 'Three Graces Piano.'

Design is critical to the success of any business, book, or good season brochure and TRIAD Communications / Next Level Interactive has excelled at enhancing Tuesday Musical's image through their excellent creative work.

The *Akron Beacon Journal* saved Tuesday Musical more than once, and we remain grateful. We thank the John S. & James L. Knight Foundation, which has provided continuing support, a tradition started by Clara I. Knight, who loved attending Tuesday Musical concerts and who remained a strong supporter throughout her life. We must also thank the GAR Foundation for providing Tuesday Musical challenge grants and continuing support.

Tuesday Musical could not present the caliber of concerts it does without E. J. Thomas Performing Arts Hall, and we applaud The University of Akron for sharing the stage with us. We also want to thank the herculean efforts of The University of Akron Press for everything it has done to bring this book to publication.

We also thank our collective community—from subscribers to foundations, businesses, and government agencies—their support continues to inspire and direct us. And, last but not least, we thank our Tuesday Musical members, past and present, whose contributions to the infrastructure of this organization year after year are too innumerable to count.

Barbara Feld

The History

Thomas Bacher

The Music Starts

THE AUTUMN OF 1887 was extremely dry in Akron, Ohio. Little rain had fallen for months and temperatures were well above normal. In some cases, livestock had to be herded for miles to find drinking water. Crops were perishing and farmers predicted a grim harvest. Across the Midwest, forest fires raged and water was sold by the barrel. A federal government report about Ohio's agricultural output noted that the general drought "has materially damaged corn and potato crops. The prospect of the apple crop is worse than ever, and more than one-fourth of the average yield cannot be expected." (*Springfield Daily Republic*, August 19, 1887).

The threat of uncontrollable flames was on citizens' minds. Akron had four fire stations equipped with four steamers, four horse-drawn hose carriages, and thirty-five firemen, but blazes typically spread rapidly across wooden structures. Gertrude Ferguson Penfield and Franklin Augustus (F. A.) Seiberling knew all about the devastation of fire. Earlier that year, a blaze had destroyed the Seiberling Empire Works building, killing one and severely injuring three employees. However, on October 12 the couple was preoccupied with something else, a wedding—their wedding. Perhaps the betrothed had talked about plans at Harriet (Hattie) Seiberling's wedding to Lucius C. Miles earlier that year, at which Gertrude was a bridesmaid. The Western Reserve erudite class, after all, associated with one another frequently. The marriage of F. A. Seiberling and Gertrude Penfield reflected a match of families who had grasped the entrepreneurial spirit—Gertrude's late father had built a clay and tile enterprise and F. A.'s father was an inventor and manufacturer of farm machinery.

Gertrude was a recent graduate of the exclusive Lasell Seminary for Young Women, a highly respected two-year college on a broad leafy campus in Auburndale, Massachusetts, near Boston. The school's purpose was to create "the 'atmosphere of culture' conducive to the training of girls for their distinctive duties in home life" (Alexander Hogg, *The Railroad as an Element in Education,* Louisville: Morton and Company, 1897). The seminary's board was $250 per year, tuition was $60 to $90 per year for the regular courses, and tuition for the music courses ranged from $60 to $150 per year. The school's musical department had seven square grand pianos, a concert grand piano, and a two-manual pipe organs, with full sets of pedals. (*American Journal of Education*, vol. 5, 1880.) Gertrude was one of five Penfield sisters who, along with a cousin and a sister-in-law, attended Lasell. Courses taught at the seminary included vocal music and instrumentation, as well as the liberal arts and the arts of domestic life. Academically, Lasell was a perfect setting for Gertrude's formative years in music and her training would help her grow an organization that had its beginnings on November 9, 1887, less than a month after the Seiberling-Penfield nuptials.

Entertainment would be part of the wedding in Willoughby, but it was unlikely that the bride sang, though she had the talent. The groom's hometown of Akron, like other towns and cities in Ohio in the late 1800s, had its gathering venues, including the Academy of Music (five hundred seats) and the Phoenix Opera House (a thousand seats). Concerts and theater productions were regularly scheduled. Vaudeville shows with knife eaters and chain benders were part of the entertainment picture, too. Akron saloons, four for every thousand residents, provided another outlet for the populace. The city had begun to prosper after 1840, when the opening of the Ohio & Erie Canal made Akron a milling location for farmers' crops, but commerce along the waterway was being replaced by trains, shrinking the time and distance between Akron and other places in the widening country.

Judging from Gertrude's character, prior to the wedding she was probably a member of a social club or two. Women met in parlors, churches, and other meetinghouses across the country. Until the late nineteenth century, these clubs were primarily devoted to self-improvement and cultural activities. Clubwomen read books, listened to lectures, and hosted musical events. Among the Ohio clubs were the Cleveland's Conversational Club, Dayton's Friday Afternoon Club, Cincinnati's Nomad Club, and Akron's Art and History Club.

After Gertrude and her new husband left on their honeymoon, an acquaintance, Celia Baker—wife of George Baker, a prominent businessman who was president of Akron Electric Light and Power—invited a select group of women with "proven musical ability" to her accommodating home at 610 East Market Street. Clearly Celia Baker, whose own musical interests contributed to the life of the First Congregational Church of Akron, had carefully selected the group. The women were to discuss ways to advance the appreciation of music in Akron and provide a performance outlet for women in the area.

On the day of the meeting, temperatures were in the mid to upper forties and the talk of the town revolved around the previous day's state elections. Republican Governor Foraker won his second term, but the Ohio legislature was to be run by a Democratic majority. Even though the women's suffrage movement was growing, the ladies who came together on East Market Street weren't eligible to vote in the 1887 Ohio elections. The women probably arrived in carriages or perhaps a few walked to the Baker residence. (See map on page 90–91 with attendees' residences.)

Historical accounts differ as to the exact number of participants at the inaugural gathering. Most records indicate that including the hostess, in attendance were Zelle Adams, Sybil Caskey, Lucy Ione Edgerton, Martha Herrold, Alma Little, Harriet Miles, Sadie (Sarah E.) Motz, Jessie Otis, Frances Robinson, and Lillie May Saunders. Many in the group, if not all, had met each other previously; some even went to elementary school together. If the women didn't know each other, most of their husbands or fathers had crossed paths.

Alma Little (married Harvey Sylvester App of Cleveland in 1895) and Ione Edgerton, whose father, Sidney, had served as a US Congressman, were both graduates of Oberlin College. Little gave music lessons in Akron, and Edgerton went on to teach music at Buchtel College and was granted an advanced music degree from Oberlin's Conservatory of Music in 1893. Sybil Caskey (married William Fair, a Cleveland veterinarian, in June 1894), the daughter of the late restaurant owner, J. G. Caskey, taught piano and theory at Buchtel College. Frances Robinson, whose father owned a business that manufactured sewer pipes, married F. H. Adams, the cashier of the First National Bank of Akron. Robinson eventually became the president of the local Ladies Aid Society. Lillie May Saunders was the daughter of Sanford Burnham, an Ohio Legislator and member of the Board of Trustees of Buchtel College, and was married to Addison T. Saunders. Sadie Motz attended one of Akron's public schools with Harriet Seiberling and Helen Storer, who also became a member of the association. Motz's father Henry was the vice president of the Akron Cracker Company. F. A. Seiberling's uncle, Monroe, was the company's president. Motz married John H. McCrum (see page 97) who became president of the Akron Varnish Company. Jessie Otis was the wife of a prominent Akron lawyer, Edward P. Otis. Harriet Miles was the former Harriet Seiberling, sister of F. A. Seiberling. Zelle Adams was the daughter of Frank Adams, a prominent Akron businessman and member of the city's board of trade. After returning from her honeymoon, Gertrude Seiberling joined the group. The meeting's convener, Celia Baker, moved to Denver, Colorado, within the year and became involved with musical activities there.

Women in Music History

1887: Nadia Juliette Boulanger, French teacher, composer, and conductor, who influenced a generation of American composers is born.

1890: Amy Marcy Beach, the first American woman to succeed as a composer of large-scale art music, composes her Mass in E flat.

1898: Mary Wurm, a British pianist, conductor, and composer of German parentage founds a women's orchestra in Berlin.

Although the initial meeting was held on a Wednesday, the women called their organization the Tuesday Afternoon Club. It's unlikely that the first meeting had an agenda. Probably tea and pastries were served, and the participants discussed plans to meet again. No records have survived.

At the time, Akron was mocked by Clevelanders as a second rate city. A small piece ran in the May 12, 1890 *Plain Dealer* that epitomized the lack of culture Clevelanders attributed to its southern neighbor.

> The *Akron Beacon* gravely assures its readers that "'philharmonic' is the German for music loving.'" This will enlighten Akronians who thought the word was compounded from "phiddle" and "harmonica."

Changing Cleveland's attitude toward the city was only one of the obstacles the Akron ladies faced. A spirited and determined Gertrude Seiberling would show leadership during the club's early years. She would also overcome her husband's apprehension—he had remarked that T.M.C. (the name changed from Tuesday Afternoon Club to Tuesday Musical Club) stood for "trouble must come" (Akron Women's History, http://www3.uakron.edu/schlcomm/womenshistory/seiberling_g.htm).

An advance in technology also coincided with the year of the first meeting of the Tuesday Afternoon Club—Emile Berliner applied for a patent on his gramophone. Ten years earlier, Thomas Edison had patented the first practical talking machine, and he named the recording machine, the record, and the reproducing machine a phonograph, a phonogram, and a phonet, respectively. In 1885, the graphophone was invented by Prof. Graham Bell and Mr. C. S. Tainter, both working at the Volta Laboratory Association of Washington. Berliner's gramophone improved on these earlier discoveries and the invention would soon lead to the large-scale introduction of music into American households.

By January 1888, the Tuesday Afternoon Club had added a few new members to its ranks. Interestingly enough, several women who purportedly attended the first meeting were not listed as charter members of the club on a photograph from that time, including Sarah Motz, Martha Herrold, Zelle Adams, Alma Little, and Frances Robinson.

Perhaps they joined shortly after the planning affair at the Baker home. The new members were Belle Brooker Luxmore (Oberlin Music Conservatory graduate and local music teacher), Helen Storer, Belle Bennett (a high school student at the time), Dorothy Belle, and Emma Motz Gehring, the sister of Sarah Motz. By 1913, only four of the original members would still be active in the club—Jessie Otis, Frances Adams, Gertrude Seiberling, and Lillie May Saunders.

The Akron club's formation reflected a national trend of women organizing music clubs. In 1893, coinciding with the World's Columbian Exhibition in Chicago, Rose Fay Thomas, whose husband was the musical director for the exhibition, invited women's amateur musical clubs to the event to meet and find ways to develop joint and standardized programming. Several years later in 1898, a number of women who had been delegates to the 1893 gathering organized the National Federation of Women's Musical Clubs under the presidency of Mrs. Edwin F. Uhl of Grand Rapids, Michigan. The organization was chartered and incorporated by the state of Illinois. The next year, the organization held its First Biennial Convention in St. Louis, Missouri, at which four regional vice presidents were appointed and four national committees created. In October of the same year, a constitution and set of bylaws were adopted. Helen Storer of Akron attended the 1893 and 1898 events, and her experiences would prove pivotal in the development of Tuesday Musical.

Ohio reflected the national movement of musical club formation. Musical clubs were organized in Cleveland, Lima, Dayton, Sandusky, Tiffin, Zanesville, and other localities. Newspapers of the era listed many of the individual clubs' events, and the Sandusky branch seemed to be one of the more active clubs, possibly due to the fact that it was in proximity to Cedar Point, which was becoming the Coney Island of the Midwest. By 1888, the resort near Sandusky had a grand pavilion, featuring an auditorium, bandstand, bowling alleys, and dining facilities. While undoubtedly not a destination for the masses, resorts and entertainment were becoming a growing part of the American landscape.

After the club's formation, several members were noted for their performances. One of the earlier mentions was the recognition of the Tuesday Afternoon Club, accompanied by Sadie Motz and Ione Edgerton, at the November 1888 grand charity concert held in Akron. As a celebration to signal the end of the Spanish-American War, the recently renamed Tuesday Musical Club, with a chorus of two hundred voices, took part in the peace celebration on Thanksgiving Day 1898. Gertrude Seiberling was the vocalist at the Cleveland Conservatory of Music's April 1899 concert. Much of the club's work and presentation, however, were undoubtedly smaller affairs held in the members' homes.

With a national organization to support women's musical clubs in place, the Akron group met with Akron notary James W. Hoffert, a law student at the Allen & Cobbs law firm, accompanied by their own representative, Joseph Kelley, who worked at the Goodrich Company, to seek incorporation on August 31, 1899. The club was represented by Lottie M. Houghton, whose husband Harry was an Akron banker; Helen Storer; Bessie Raymond, whose father, William B. helped fund the Citizens' Savings and Loan Association of Akron; and Harriet Miles, whose husband, Lucius went on to become vice president of the Goodyear Tire and Rubber Company. Storer, who was an 1890 graduate of Wellesley College and held a degree in music with a specialty in organ and harmony, became director (the terms director and president were used interchangeably for several years) of Akron's Tuesday Musical Club and Cleveland's Fortnightly Club, and was elected president of the National Federation of Music Clubs in 1903.

The incorporating document described the club as intended "for the study and rendition of music, to organize and maintain a school for instruction and cultivation in vocal and instrumental music and to acquire and hold funds and property convenient therefore" (Ohio Secretary of State, Document No. A041_1748, 1901). The act of incorporation was evidence that interest in becoming a member of Tuesday Musical Club was growing. Forty women counted themselves as participants, and the club held modest recitals and performed at other events in the city. The club touted a woman's chorus and a mixed chorus.

On January 30, 1901, the state of Ohio registered the filing for Tuesday Musical Club as a non-profit corporation. The *Akron Beacon Journal* reported the event and indicated that the incorporation came without "capitalization" and was done by the club to "put it upon a strict business basis" (January 30, 1901). At the time, Akron, whose population was in excess of 50,000, listed eighteen music teachers, five musical instrument retailers, and five piano tuners in the city directory. Four bands were listed—the Eighth Regiment band, Foster's Band, the Goodrich band, and the K.O.T.M. (Knights of the Maccabees) band. The town had two orchestras, Mustill's and Stickle's, an opera house on North Main Street, a musician's union, and two organizations of German heritage, the Akron Liedertafel and the Akron Saengerbund, that emphasized music training and performance.

Akron's Academy of Music, a massive brick Romanesque building on the northeast corner of Main and Market Streets was the home to many concerts, some undoubtedly by the local bands and orchestras. Built in 1871 by John F. Seiberling, the academy was described as "the neatest and handsomest place of public amusement in the country" (Jack Gieck, *Early Akron's Industrial Valley*, Kent State University Press, 2007). The academy was heavily damaged in 1878 in a blaze called "the most formidable fire of the season" (Samuel Lane, *Fifty Years and Over of Akron and Summit County*, Akron, OH: Beacon Job Department, 1892). The building was remodeled and reopened in 1879 with new opera seats, steam heating, and gas lighting. Three Bell telephones that connected directly to the local fire department were installed in the building, as well as a water tank and a hose to aid in the dousing of flames. On October 29, 1889, John F. and Frank A. Seiberling exchanged the Academy of Music block, valued at $100,000, for a controlling interest in the Akron Electric Street Railroad (*Hillsboro News-Herald*, November 7, 1889). F. A. might have been divesting himself of the entertainment business, but Gertrude was working to increase the presence and performances of Tuesday Musical.

A New Century

AT THE TURN OF the twentieth century, a *Ladies Home Journal* article predicted what might happen by the year 2000. Some of the ideas were quite revolutionary—wireless global voice communication and television images that would be available to viewers anywhere on earth. Others were a bit unique—'C,' 'X,' or 'Q' would be dropped from the everyday alphabet and mail delivery would be accomplished by pneumatic tubes spanning hundreds of miles. The article also forecast changes in how listeners would be treated to music.

> Grand Opera will be telephoned to private homes, and will sound as harmonious as though enjoyed from a theatre box. Automatic instruments reproducing original airs exactly will bring the best music to the families of the untalented. Great musicians gathered in one enclosure in New York will, by manipulating electric keys, produce at the same time music from instruments arranged in theatres or halls in San Francisco or New Orleans, for instance. Thus will great bands and orchestras give long-distance concerts. In great cities there will be public opera-houses whose singers and musicians are paid from funds endowed by philanthropists and by the government. The piano will be capable of changing its tone from cheerful to sad. Many devises will add to the emotional effect of music. (*Ladies Home Journal*, December 1900)

It's not out of the question that members of Tuesday Musical Club read about the future expectations, but they were definitely concerned with the business at hand.

Others in Akron might have been excited about the new skating rink that was to open New Year's Day 1900, at the corner of East Market and

Kirkwood Streets. Reports of a strange, ghostly illumination in front of a burial vault at Union Cemetery also circulated. Some residents were making plans to attend the Militaer Verein's annual New Year's Celebration, featuring hot wine punch. With the forecast calling for snow, residents would need to bundle up.

During the Gay Nineties, Tuesday Musical continued to show rapid progress in serving the community. In 1894, under the direction of the club's president Helen Storer, the club expanded its activities. The woman's chorus expanded to include male voices and rehearsed in the evening. Conductors were recruited, such as a Professor Gustave Sigel of Buchtel College, Dr. George W. Andrews, the first conductor of the Oberlin Conservatory of Music Orchestra, and James H. Rogers, the well-regarded composer, choirmaster, and organist of Cleveland's Euclid Avenue Temple and First Unitarian Church.

Two years later, the men were performing as an all-male chorus. In the meantime, the club's study section continued to meet on Tuesday afternoons to pursue the group's educational goals. At these events, members presented papers and talks on various musical topics and held chamber concerts. The first evening concert programs began in 1895, consisting of modest offerings known as the Evening Artists' Concert Courses.

Entrance to the ranks of Tuesday Musical involved skill and talent. To become a member, vocalists had to perform an aria or oratorio and four additional songs; pianists, violinists, and other instrumentalists were required to play a Beethoven sonata, a Chopin etude and nocturne, and three pieces from other famous composers; accompanists, after taking the required examination, also had to play two songs by sight while accompanying a soloist who was a member of the examining committee. Even with strict membership requirements, Tuesday Musical continued to grow. The irony was that the economic climate during the time was less than favorable.

The country experienced a financial meltdown in 1893. During that year, the stock market collapsed and over fifteen thousand businesses failed—including major railroads like the Northern Pacific and

Union Pacific. Locally, John Seiberling lost his factories and fortune. Ferdinand Schumacher, the oatmeal king, overextended his ventures and lost his holdings. Unemployment rates soared to 25 percent in the United States and in Ohio reached as high as 50 percent among industrial workers. By 1897, the economic situation had stabilized, but Akron industrialists would continue to face tough times into the next century. Contributing to the economic upheaval, the city of Akron itself was facing a large debt and was forced to issue bonds to cover expenses.

Perhaps Tuesday Musical's growth was spurred on because the 1890s were a significant decade for the emergence of the commercial popular music industry in the United States. Sales of sheet music, which allowed individuals to play and sing popular songs in their own parlors, rose prodigiously during the Gay Nineties, led by Tin Pan Alley, the narrow street in midtown Manhattan that housed the country's major music publishers and producers. The key development came in 1892 when Charles K. Harris's "After the Ball," a sentimental love tune, sold two million pieces of sheet music that year alone and went on to sell over five million copies.

One getaway, for those who could afford the luxury, were the concerts by Tuesday Musical. In February 1900, the club presented Mendelssohn's *Elijah* and the *Akron Beacon Journal* called the event "an artistic triumph" (February 22, 1900). Later that same month, a chamber concert was held in the afternoon. These smaller musical shows, along with the instructions offered at them, were the "chief delight of the ladies' of the club" (*Akron Beacon Journal,* May 23, 1900). Since the president at the time, Helen Storer, also held the same position with Cleveland's Fortnightly Club, Tuesday Musical invited that club to Akron. On April 4, twenty-five members from the Cleveland club arrived at the union depot "before the luncheon hour" for a social gathering and concert (*Akron Beacon Journal,* April 4,1900). The final concert of the season was held at the auditorium of the First Methodist Church in late May and featured local talent only. A few days previously, Storer, who was getting married, resigned as the president of the

Akron and Cleveland clubs. Harriet Parsons, whose voice was sweet and vibrant with beauty, was elected president, and the club honored Storer with a silver toilet set.

The club had been using churches, including the Methodist and Baptist churches of Akron, for larger affairs and individual homes for smaller concerts, but the club's membership continued to grow. The ladies were looking for a larger venue for the club and a local retailer, C. H. Martin, was able to provide the needed space. Martin sold pianos out of his storefront in the Walsh block on 159 South Main Street. He also invented a unique piano bench around 1914 that had a cabinet for music storage incorporated as part of the design. Martin's original business would go into receivership in late 1900, but he would reopen in 1906 at 24 West Market Street under the name of E. J. Martin.

According to the *Akron Beacon Journal*, the hall would be on "the second floor from the Main street entrance and is reached by elevator or stairs. It is on the east side of the building, removed from the noise of Main Street, and on the ground level in the rear. It has excellent means of ventilation, light and heat. Mr. Martin expects to make it a complete little hall with 200 comfortable chairs, a good-sized stage and dressing room" (July 14, 1900). The additional space was vital to the expansion of Tuesday Musical Club because, as the newspaper noted, "Akron has attained the reputation of being a musical city where the best musicians can come before appreciative audiences."

The clubroom above the failed Martin business would continue to be used by Tuesday Musical for musical programs and auditions, but by the fall of the 1900 season, the evening concerts were too well subscribed. The Pittsburgh Orchestra performed in the Methodist church in early November, providing a concert that "suited all tastes." The orchestra was late in arriving due to delays on the Lake Shore Railroad, but the audience "bore this delay good naturedly" (*Akron Beacon Journal*, November 15, 1900). The year ended with the third annual rendition of Handel's *Messiah* with one hundred and fifty members of the club as part of the chorus.

In 1901, Charles E. Clemens of Cleveland was appointed musical director of Tuesday Musical, indicating that the club had gained a distinct and growing reputation outside of Summit County. Considering how Clevelanders viewed Akron, the appointment was a bit of a coup. Clemens had been the organist at St. Paul's Church in Cleveland and was a lecturer and organist at Western Reserve University. He was born in Davenport, England, and had spent almost a decade in Berlin under the patronage of Empress Friedrich. Tireless at his task, he was fond of saying, "rest is merely a change of occupation" (*American Organist*, vol. 2, no. 7, July 1919).

Word obviously spread of Clemens's background. In September, at the club's first rehearsal for the upcoming season, a record number of club members attended. Further, twelve new voices were on hand to seek admission to the club.

The program for the coming season promised to be the best the club had ever offered. The highlight of the season was the April 1902 concert that featured Madame Schumann-Heink. Schumann-Heink, a world-famous Wagnerian contralto, reputedly earned $135,000 a year in concert fees. (The average US worker made between $200 and $400 annually in the early 1900s.) She appeared regularly at the New York Metropolitan Opera, Carnegie Hall, and at other major venues around the country.

The March concert was to be a night of grand opera featuring Herbert Witherspoon, who would go onto become the first basso at the Metropolitan Opera. He began his career in Henry W. Savage's Castle Opera Company. Among his accomplishments were the parts of Ramfis in *Aida*, Colline in *La Bohème*, and Henry I in *Lohengrin*.

The organization continued with its afternoon recitals and evening study and performance sections. Clemens performed at one of the afternoon events on piano, an instrument he had also studied. The club indicated that it was spending over twice the amount it had previously to secure better talent. The evening concert series was the backbone of the club's income and bringing Schumann-Heink and Witherspoon, along with the Pittsburgh Orchestra and the Singer's

Club of Cleveland, was sure to generate ticket sales, but the club was now facing a new competitor—the Colonial Theater.

Women in Music History

1908: Dutch composer and conductor Elisabeth Kuyper became the first woman to teach theory and composition at the Berlin Hochschule für Musik.

1912: At a time when nearly all major symphony orchestras were exclusively male, Henry Wood admits four women, including the violist/composer Rebecca Clarke, into the New Queen's Hall Orchestra.

1918: Music patron Elizabeth Sprague Coolidge founds the South Mountain Chamber Music Festival (later the Berkskhire Music Festival), an important summer festival for chamber music.

Two Akron insurance agents, W. W. McIntosh and William C. Hall, teamed up with Horace B. Camp, an engineer and inventor, to finance the construction of a downtown entertainment venue that opened on March 2, 1902. The Colonial's first offering was a performance of the light opera, *Floradora*, and the *Akron Beacon Journal* noted "never before has such a crowd gathered in an Akron playhouse" (March 3, 1902). The event was standing room only, with lower level and balcony seating tickets priced between seventy-five cents and two dollars. The upper gallery seats, sold on the day of the event, went for fifty cents. After the premier, thirty street cars were lined up on Mill and Main Streets to transport theatergoers to their homes. The Colonial became the leading playhouse in Akron and would remain so until the days of vaudeville and road shows ended.

In late May 1902, Tuesday Musical released information on the 1903 concert season. A favorite, the Pittsburgh Orchestra, would lead off on November 19. Herbert Witherspoon would return for another operatic concert. The Philharmonic String Quartet would come down from Cleveland and the last concert would be performances by club members as usual. However, the greatest excitement was the fourth in the series of concerts, which was to be given by a well-known soloist, probably performing Rossini's *Stabat Mater*. Considering the club had brought Schumann-Heink the previous season people wondered who the club would book this time, since Rossini's work required a voice of great range and was usually only performed at the world's great music centers.

The question was never answered, because on November 11, 1902, Tuesday Musical was dissolved. Bills had piled up and ticket sales had dwindled. After five years, the club was estimating a debt of $1,200 if it went on with the season. Rather than face bankruptcy and sully their image, the ladies of the club decided to cut their losses, pay off all creditors, and go ahead with the first, and ultimately, last concert of the season, which was to feature the Pittsburgh Orchestra. As J. W. Kelley, the chairman of the club, put it:

> We have worked hard to have the club a success this year, but find that the sale of tickets has been smaller than ever before and that the club would be in debt at the end of the season. Rather than have this happen and have any one lose money, we have decided that the most honorable plan would be to stop now before any one has lost money. It is a hard thing to do but we decided that it would be the more honest, and for that reason have dissolved. (*Akron Beacon Journal*, November 11, 1902)

Classical music lovers of Akron were not completely without options. The afternoon section of the club decided to continue to have members read papers on one of the great composers and to have a soloist illustrate the composition of the composers discussed. Recitals would also be given. Eventually, though, even the study section was disbanded.

The Music Returns

SPILLMAN RIGGS WAS A humorist and musical impersonator who was known for his "Musical Fits and Misfits" presentation. He began lecturing in 1890 and his popularity rose because he got hearty laughs "from the crowd often enough to chase back the tears that start at some of Riggs' pathetic tales" (Hollister Brothers, Spillman Riggs promotional brochure, 1906). In November 1902, Riggs married Akronite Minnie Etta Heneberger, whose father was a local grocer. Riggs became a booking agent, as well as a performer, and his new wife helped him with arrangements. This skill would soon become valuable to Gertrude Seiberling and Elizabeth Eyster.

Gertrude Seiberling had performed on many occasions for Tuesday Musical. Her vocal skills gained her a regional reputation, and she was the key accompanist for many club concerts. Her husband's Goodyear Company had faced a financial crisis in early 1903 and many Akron businessmen felt that the company would be forced to close. In fact on one occasion in the spring, Seiberling had to get the Hower Company, an East Akron department store, to sign a note so Goodyear could pay its employees. Luckily, in May, a favorable court decision was reached concerning a patent infringement case filed against Goodyear, freeing up escrow funds and putting Goodyear on firm financial footing. Undoubtedly, Gertrude was now more likely to rethink the prospects of bringing Tuesday Musical to life again.

The other woman who helped develop a plan to revitalize Tuesday Musical was the former Elizabeth Bolender, who had married William Eyster, the manager of the delicatessen department at the P. E. Tanner (wholesale and retail) Grocery Company. Minnie Etta Riggs' father was an area produce vendor, so perhaps Elizabeth Eyster and Minnie Etta Riggs knew each other.

The outcome of their efforts, the first meeting of the reorganized Tuesday Musical, was held on November 23, 1903. To prepare for the club's renewal, several members had arranged for Gertrude Seiberling to attend the convention of the National Federation of Musical Clubs held in Rochester, New York, in late May 1903. On her return, Seiberling helped outline a new operational scheme. The club was formally divided into two sections—an afternoon section with an emphasis on education and an evening section to administer concert programming. To increase club participation, a people's chorus, open to anyone who possessed "a fair voice and a love for music," was created (Tuesday Musical Collection, University of Akron Archives). A student membership was also inaugurated.

The connection between Akron's club and the national organization was very strong. Helen Storer Collins, an early member of the Akron group, was elected the third president of the National Federation. During her term, she worked to increase club membership in the federation, prompting 125 new clubs to join. She led the amending of the club's organizational structure to allow men to become members. She also started the federation's Artist Bureau, which allowed local clubs to get better pricing for national artists and provided for the exchange of talent by clubs in the same regional vicinity.

Gertrude Seiberling also brought back from the National Federation the idea of incorporating the National Federation's course of study within Tuesday Musical's educational offerings. The National Federation had a distinct curriculum for teaching individuals the value of classical music.

> The "Course of Study," of which this is the initial book [*The Development of the Symphony*, Thomas Whitney Surette], is designed to meet the present needs of the music students and those who desire to understand and appreciate concert programs, even though they may not be performers or active musicians.

> The majority of concert-goers do not care to delve into music history; they wish to understand the present-day program which is frequently available to them.
>
> If the concert programs of today are made clear, an interest is excited and one is stimulated to further study.
>
> Research work comes later. (*Musical Monitor*, vol. 4, no. 10, June 1915)

Most of all, however, Gertrude Seiberling and her cohorts were able to generate monetary support for the reorganized club. As the *Akron Beacon Journal* noted, "it being the assurance of several of the music lovers of the city who are in a position to lend financial assistance to the club that there will be no lack of funds with which to conduct business" (November 12, 1903). Although unnamed, the likelihood is that many of Akron's business entrepreneurs, some of whom happened to be married to ladies of the club, contributed to the well-being of Tuesday Musical. The club could again plan for a season of concerts and recitals, providing "the leaven of musical culture, of musical appreciation, of social entertainment, of enjoyment in the home, and ... [be] a power against the sordid condition that obtains in a purely commercial environment" (*Musical Monitor*, vol. 3, 1913).

Around the same time, rumors floated around the city about a merger between Tuesday Musical and Akron's Liedertafel. The German-American club was in the final stages of constructing a new music hall and the consolidation of two organizations that sponsored concerts and other musical events seemed reasonable. Paul E. Werner, an Akron newspaper publisher, printer, and industrialist financed the $65,000 building. The *Akron Daily Democrat* provided a vivid description of how the final edifice would look.

> The structure will be a very handsome one. The outside walls of the building will be of stone and yellow brick, and the roof red tile or red slate. The basement, which will be almost entirely above the ground and well lighted, will contain a large banquet hall with a convenient seating capacity of from 500 to 600; a large kitchen and storage rooms with modern equipment; a large rehearsal room with stage and such conveniences as are required for a building of this character. It will also contain equipment for a gymnasium.

> The first floor will contain large and convenient ladies' and gentleman's reception rooms; a magnificent auditorium with a seating capacity of from 1800 to 2000 persons; a stage sufficiently large for grand opera and large choruses; a modern grand concert organ, and such other conveniences as are required in this connection.
>
> The second floor will have music, library and reading rooms connected with a very convenient gallery. (*Akron Daily Democrat*, March 20, 1901)

As quickly as the idea of a merger surfaced, it was extinguished. Louis Seybold, who had been the musical director of the Akron Harmonie from 1876–79 and was the editor of *Germanie* (the local German-language newspaper), indicated that the Liedertafel would provide help to Tuesday Musical when they had time, but even though the Liedertafel "have accepted an invitation to take part in the general rehearsals of the Tuesday Musical Club, once a month, they will in no way give up or neglect their regular work or lose their identity as a society or musical organization in any sense" (*Akron Beacon Journal*, December 19, 1903).

In many respects, a union of the two groups might have ended the story of Tuesday Musical, or at the least, altered the growth of the organization, but instead the club moved forward and elected a new president, Minnie Etta Riggs, a chairman of the evening section, Professor N. L. Glover, and a chairman of the afternoon section, Ione Edgerton. In late November, the evening chorus, with its new musical director, Professor G. W. Andrews of Oberlin College, held its first meeting with around a hundred voices on hand, and about fifty more who promised to make the next session. The club wasn't in a position to put together a concert series for the city. After the previous unexpected 1902 cancellation, some Akronites were a bit hesitant to fully support Tuesday Musical Club. Much work still needed to be done.

Revelers in New York City gathered around the Old Trinity Church to usher in 1904. The crowd was so rowdy and boisterous that the organ program including "Parting Song 11:55 pm," "Auld Lang Syne," and "Home, Sweet Home," was impossible to hear. Wall Street brokers who had come to regard New Year's Eve as the biggest day of the year, since bonuses were handed out then, faced disappointment at the end of 1903. In 1902, J. P. & Morgan had given out bonuses reflecting 100 percent of an employee's salary, but due to economic trends reduced 1903 bonuses to as little as 15 percent. The start of 1904 was further darkened by the news of a massive fire in the new Iroquois Theater in Chicago that had taken the lives of nearly six hundred people.

Akron's Tuesday Musical began its activities in 1904 with an afternoon session. Mary Zipperlen Schumacher, the second wife of Akron's oatmeal king, gave a paper on the history of the pianoforte and Grace Barager presented on composers for the piano. The *Akron Beacon Journal* reprinted Schumacher's paper in its Thursday edition, beginning a partnership that would help the club at the end of 1905. Mary Schumacher, whose marriage to Ferdinand came as a surprise to Akronites in 1899, would do even more to keep the club afloat.

A few weeks later on the 13th, the afternoon section met again at 578 East Market Street, the house of Julia C. Houser. Houser's husband Horace was the treasurer and manager of the Akron Cultivator Company, a manufacturer of among other items, wheelbarrows, and the couple's house was one of the few in Akron at the time that had a Bell telephone. As usual a program was given. However, the meeting was focused on "working for the success of the evening section, arranging for concerts, selling tickets to the same and getting a list of guarantors" (*Akron Beacon Journal*, January 13, 1904). At the time the club had 115 benefactors and was aiming to reach two hundred.

On March 30 at Akron's M.E. Church, Tuesday Musical held its first evening concert since its reorganization. The star of the show was Lillian Blauvelt, an American singer from Brooklyn, New York, who preferred to be called Mademoiselle Blauvelt. Blauvelt had a world famous reputation, performing operas in Paris, Milan, and Brussels. Bringing such a talent to Akron was remarkable for fine music patrons—who turned out in large numbers for the event. The concertgoers also were entertained by the club's two hundred-voice chorus.

The rebirth of Tuesday Musical also heightened the anticipation that Akronites must have felt for the planned opening of the soon-to-be completed German-American Music Hall located on East Exchange

Street. The center piece of the hall was a grand organ pipe organ that cost $12,500 and was being built by the eminent Lyon & Healy Company of Chicago. Some premonition concerning the manufacturing of the instrument had to be in the air because the Chicago concern was facing a strike at the time, but in the end, the organ, a three manual instrument of forty-six speaking stops, twelve couplers, and thirty-five mechanical accessories was in place for the opening. Among the backers who made the purchase and installation of the organ possible was Minnie Etta Riggs, the president of Tuesday Musical. (The great organ wouldn't be completely paid off for months and ladies of the German-American Club held several fund-raising events to generate the necessary cash.)

The opening concert, held on September 15, 1904, was headlined by Victor Herbert and his orchestra. Herbert was the former conductor of the Pittsburgh Orchestra, a frequent performing group at Tuesday Musical events. Herbert was also the musical advisor to the Edison Phonograph Works. Befitting the occasion, Akron Mayor C. W. Kempel, Judge J. A. Kohler, president of the People's Savings Bank of Akron, and Paul Werner, president of the Akron Saengerfest and the hall's benefactor, made remarks at the event.

The intertwined nature of business relationships of the Akron elite was evident. Kohler was a partner in Giant Oil Production Company, which controlled three thousand acres of land near Lima, Ohio. Among the other investors were Akron bankers L. C. Miller and J. S. Banner, and Akron retired capitalist, J. F. Seiberling. The opening crowd was undoubtedly made up of the wealthier members of the community. This perception would add to Tuesday Musical's woes later the next year.

An added benefit for Tuesday Musical was the new music hall recital room, large and roomy without being too large, that became the organization's new quarters and was on full display at the club's September 20 evening session. The accommodations must have given the ladies of the club a renewed energy to continue the programs they were offering to the community. Paul Werner greeted the club members and offered them an apology for failing to recognize the club as one of the organizations that had funded a gift to him on the opening of the music hall. He went on to compliment them for their contributions to the music hall's opening and wished them prosperity in their new surroundings.

Making use of the recital hall, the first event, held on September 27, was sponsored by the afternoon section and featured Madame Cara Revillio, 'The Norwegian Nightingale.' Single admission tickets were sold at the door for fifty cents. Other events planned included a November lecture and piano recital by Nellie Cook, a graduate of the Leipzig and Vienna conservatories; a January lecture by Arthur Farwell, an ardent supporter of American music and founder of the American Music Society; and a program of Wagnerian music offered by pianist Herman O. C. Kortheur. If a special event was not scheduled, the afternoon section still met on Tuesdays at 1:30 pm to continue the study plan of the National Federation of Music Clubs and vote on candidates who wanted to become active members.

Tuesday Musical was a volunteer organization; members did not receive payment for working on programs, scheduling concerts, or selling tickets. Prior to the 1920s, if a woman was employed, she usually left the workforce after marriage. Some women were professionals, often teachers or clerical workers, but a substantial social stigma existed for wives working outside the home. Faced with this environment, volunteering was the best avenue to extend interests and engage in social activities. Still, volunteerism had its limits. Near the end of October 1904, Frances S. Marvin, a widow, resigned from her position as assistant conductor of the club. She cited the great amount of time required, especially the work outside of regular club activities to become familiar with the many choruses sung by members. She couldn't afford the extra hours. Her duties were turned over to Professor N. L. Glover, a local music instructor, and the club moved forward.

By this time, the club followed an annual routine of electing its officers for the afternoon and evening sections during May of a given year and then planning for the upcoming season, which roughly stretched from fall through spring. Having access to the National Federation's

Artist Bureau made booking talent easier and artists themselves could give performances in a shorter period of time in neighboring cities—perhaps Pittsburgh, Akron, Cleveland, and Chicago. The last two concerts of 1904 sponsored by Tuesday Musical brought Emil Paur, the leader of the Pittsburgh Symphony Orchestra, and Luigi von Kunits, the accomplished violinist, for a performance, and Madame Maconda, well-known for her operatic vocal range and the rich quality of her singing.

The end of 1904 started with a new tradition for the country. The New York Times Company, celebrating its move to midtown Manhattan, sponsored a celebration and fireworks show in Longacre Square (soon to be renamed Times Square). The inaugural event brought two hundred thousand revelers to the city, and would be repeated every year. Folks west of Akron—especially in places like Wisconsin—weren't likely to be celebrating, since they were facing up to twenty-six inches of snow. The local Saalfield Publishing Company was advertising its titles in the *Bookseller* magazine—including the popular Billy Whiskers series, which told the comical tales of a pet goat, or the new title from Mary Agnes Bryne, *The Little Dame Trot*. The books surely were wrapped as Christmas presents for some Akron youngsters.

Tuesday Musical continued its programs and concerts during the spring of 1905. Before the May election, Minnie Etta Riggs indicated that she didn't want to continue her role as president. Perhaps the treasurer's report, showing the club to be in debt in the amount of $500, was at issue. After Riggs was persuaded to continue, the members were relieved to hear that Paul Werner would help the club by paying the remaining amounts the club owed for the organ and recital hall rentals at the German-American Hall. Finances, however, needed further discussion. A proposition to raise the dues from two to three dollars and require members to sell four season tickets each year was not adopted, but the club did decide to limit the concerts for the upcoming season to three instead of four.

Riggs' presidency would last less than two weeks. She formally resigned, indicating she "was worn out from the two years of increasing work for the club, and needs a complete rest" (*Akron Beacon Journal*, May 26, 1905). Perhaps there were some internal policy squabbles among board members or perhaps Riggs's ongoing medical issues required her to quit. The club elected Jessie Otis, one of the women who met in 1887 to form the club, as the new president. Otis indicated she would undertake her duties "with a businesslike, conservative policy," book the best talent available—finances permitting—and seek to increase the number of backers for the club (*Akron Beacon Journal*, May 26, 1905). The club could not continue to subsidize performances and needed to ensure that ticket sales covered expenses.

In September, the afternoon section announced its program for autumn, but plans were still being made for the evening concert series. The regular plan of study, which had been in place for the two previous years, was discontinued in favor of afternoon sessions that would cover one specific topic completely. This arrangement was instituted in hopes that more individuals, including associate members and evening session subscribers who paid a small fee to come to afternoon events, would attend. Unfortunately, the public at large did not come out to support either the evening concerts or afternoon recitals. In December, due to lack of support, the club's chorus was disbanded. The evening concert that was to feature the Lohengrin opera was cancelled.

The club's officers detailed the situation in a letter to the *Akron Beacon Journal*.

> To the Editor:
>
> A statement to the guarantors and the other 238 who are interested in music in Akron.
>
> The premature announcement of the disbanding of the chorus of the Tuesday Musical club has doubtless been the cause of much conjecture since last night. ... The year of work began with a debt of $500 which the members of the club reduced to $300 last year. ... Expenses were reduced in every way possible. The revenue of the club comes from the payment of annual dues from the members and from the sale of season tickets. Last year being the first opportunity to see the new Music hall, the number of seats sold was very large viz., 1,200.

> The board figured at least on selling 1,000 seats this year. The revenue from this would have left $400 in the treasury after all expenses for the year had been met. ... Instead of 1,000 or even 800 seats being sold, which would cover the actual expenses there are 438 paid seats in the auditorium, the remaining 100 being held by active members at the opening concert.
>
> From a population of 50,000 there are only 438 persons who love music and who appreciate the educational value such as this club is to the chorus and members of the study section. It looks as if the time had come to cease collecting patronage of an uninterested public. (December 3, 1905)

The *Akron Beacon Journal* also admonished Akronites for their lack of support of Tuesday Musical, an organization the newspaper called "one of the best known" in the country. Hyperbolic in its tone, the paper's editorial went on to say that if financial support did not come, "great treats that were in store for Akron people will not be realized after all." Perhaps the populace had grown tired of the "plethora of musical stars ... and ... too many concerts and attractions" (*Akron Beacon Journal,* December 15, 1905). The paper took it upon itself to sponsor a fund to save the club by donating twenty-five dollars to the cause and asking individuals and businesses to do so in increments as small as a dollar. Tuesday Musical needed $1,000 to make the final two concerts of the year a reality, and according to the *Beacon*, the club was "one of the institutions that the city [couldn't] afford to [let] die" (*Akron Beacon Journal,* December 16, 1905).

One can only imagine the discussions that took place in the Seiberling, Otis, Miles, and Wannamaker households. The same conversations were likely held in other Akron homes of club members. The nagging question of being a second-rate city in the shadow of Cleveland and Pittsburg reappeared. F. A. Seiberling, A. H. Noah, treasurer of the Diamond Rubber Company, and Paul Werner sent in a hundred dollars each. (Note: a dollar in 1905 would be worth about twenty-six dollars in 2013.) The Akron mayor sent in ten dollars, the proprietor of the Summit House Hotel contributed five dollars, and a Goodrich worker added a dollar. However, just a few days before Christmas, the fund was well short of the amount needed to keep renowned musicians performing as part of Tuesday Musical's programs.

While the *Akron Beacon Journal* was working to raise funds, a dispute arose fostered by an editorial and anonymous letter in the rival *Akron Times-Democrat*. The *Times-Democrat* accused Tuesday Musical of being an organization of and for the wealthy members of Akron, hostile to all other music groups in the city, and used by officers of the club for their personal gain. The *Beacon Journal* reaffirmed its support of Tuesday Musical, vilifying the *Times-Democrat* not only for spreading nearly libelous falsehoods, but doing so behind the cloak of anonymity. Two Tuesday Musical chorus members, D. F. Owens, a local grocer, and E. T. Jones, an Akron tailor, sent a response that was printed in the *Beacon Journal,* pointing out that a quick look at the club's roster showed that "people in every walk of life are members of this society and all are welcomed into its fold" (December 23, 1905).

As the city celebrated the new year, the required funds, however, still had not been raised. Of the amount needed, $710 had been donated by January 4, 1906. The *Akron Beacon Journal* kept imploring its readers to ensure nineteen years of labor by members of the club would not be wasted. The community had only a few more days to keep the organization afloat and ensure that the two remaining concerts would be held. As the paper noted, concerts given by Tuesday Musical could not be heard "in ordinary cases for less than $5 each but the club has fixed matters so that they can be heard for 75 cents each, just a little more than the price of gallery seats at the best attractions at local theaters" (January 5, 1906). The final push worked, the city was saved the disgrace of being deemed a city without culture, and the paper thanked those "citizens who heeded the call" (*Akron Beacon Journal*, January 8, 1906).

Shortly after, Tuesday Musical held a special meeting. The club's president Jessie Otis predicted a brilliant future for the club because the attacks by the *Times-Democrat* had been thwarted. Gertrude Seiberling, in her role as director of programming, echoed Otis's sentiments and indicated the club had identified a number of local music people who were not club members. A committee including Jessie Otis, Gertrude Seiberling, and G. C. Donaldson was formed to contact these nonmembers and other individuals to increase participation. As a marketing initiative, new members would only be charged $1.50 to join and their membership would include two tickets to the remaining concerts.

These efforts probably had an effect on the club's ranks, but the rubber business was also beginning to expand, resulting in a steady increase in the local population and a large cash flow into the city. In the late 1890s, rubber companies found a strong market in making tires for bicycles. The bicycle craze lasted into the early twentieth century, when cars began to become popular. Akron entrepreneurs, realizing that the very successful Goodrich Company was the only rubber manufacturer in the western part of the nation, started competing companies. The Diamond Rubber Company was formed and took over the old Diamond Match buildings. Using an abandoned strawboard factory, the Goodyear Tire and Rubber Company started manufacturing in 1898. Harvey Firestone, formerly a buggy salesman in Detroit, founded the Firestone Tire and Rubber Company at the turn of the twentieth century.

In 1904, the United States surpassed France as the largest auto producer and between 1904 and 1908, 240 firms were established in the US to manufacture cars. In 1908, Goodrich posted sales of $14 million, but by 1911, sales had reached $27.5 million. Firestone saw its sales increase from $7.5 million in 1911 to $25 million in 1915. Goodyear's sales went from $25 million in 1912 to $168 million in 1919.

Akron's population skyrocketed, too. When the twentieth century began, 42,000 people lived in the city. By 1910, the population had almost doubled. In 1920, the population reached 208,000 residents. In 1907, the city directory listed six automobile manufacturers. In 1914, the number grew to eleven. Only thirty-three restaurants were serving meals in 1907. By 1914, seventy-two dining establishments could be found in Akron, not to mention the scores of lunch rooms around the city.

The growth of Akron had a great deal to do with the financial stability of Tuesday Musical. While many new residents were laborers at tire manufacturers and the secondary industries that grew up around the rubber plants, managerial and other executive positions also showed marked growth. Certainly, Tuesday Musical accepted members who had musical talent, but the fixed seating capacity (the music hall could seat two thousand), coupled with a rapid growth in potential subscribers, made concert revenue more certain, a relief to the ladies of the club.

Singing Out

EVAN WILLIAMS ONCE SAID, "It isn't true that my boyhood days in the coal mines were weighed down by poverty ... I was rich then. I was a big strong fellow and I got man's wages and I had as many good times and took as many buggy rides as anybody in East Akron" (*The Cambrian*, vol. 38, no. 11, June 1918). Williams was born in 1867 to Welsh parents in Mineral Ridge, Ohio. He was three when his mother died while giving birth to his brother Joseph. The boys were sent to live with their aunt, Sarah Davis, and her husband, Thomas, in the Welsh mining community of Thomastown near Akron, where he met and married his wife Margaret. By then his vocal ability had been discovered at a Welsh Eisteddfod and he was paid two dollars each Sunday to be part of the choir at Akron's Methodist Church. He began his rise through the American music ranks, getting positions as a singer at several churches, performing domestically and internationally, and making records. At one time, his earnings were only exceeded by two other tenors of his era—Enrico Caruso and John McCormack. Even as his fame reached around the globe, Williams felt a deep commitment to Akron and eventually built a $100,000 home on Mayfield Road.

Williams contributed greatly to Tuesday Musical. In many ways a self-made star, Williams had a keen perception of his voice quality and knew how to ensure he could perform at his best. This led him to develop four postulates to maintain his mastery: tone creates its own support; much of the time spent in elaborate breathing exercises do not produce the results expected; the singer's first studies should be with his brain and ear, rather than through an attempt at muscular control of the breathing muscles; and vocal resonance can be developed through a proper understanding of tone color so that uniformly excellent production of tones will result (*The Etude*, September 1927).

Under his direction, Akron's club took part in the mixed chorus section of the 1906 Stark County Eisteddfod competition. The competition was hailed by the *Stark County Democrat* as an event that would surpass any Eisteddfod held anywhere else in the United States (*Stark County Democrat*, June 12, 1906) and four thousand visitors came from several states to hear the choruses and individual performers. The Tuesday Musical chorus faced groups from Cleveland, Pittsburgh, and Utica, New York, as well as several other areas. Williams' training must have worked, since the Akron mixed chorus took home the gold medal and a cash award of $600.

The victory was somewhat of a surprise considering the members' reactions. The ladies of the club couldn't keep from showing their admiration and flocked to the stage, surrounding Williams. They rousingly congratulated him, and in a show of emotion that was not common during the era, several ladies "kissed Mr. Williams" (*Stark County Democrat*, July 6, 1906).

After the Canton event, Williams gave a concert in Akron and later that same year was made an honorary member of Tuesday Musical. The club was also recognized for its role in bringing culture to the populace. And, perhaps best of all, the club treasurer reported that it was very likely the club would end the season without a deficit. Being in the black must have given the ladies of Tuesday Musical a wonderful outlook for the coming year, an outlook that was shared by the three thousand BF Goodrich employees who got a New Year's gift of a 5 percent increase in wages.

The club's stability was less of a problem and the value of the club was continuing to grow, again supported in part by the *Akron Beacon Journal*. A February 1907 story emphasized the club's motto, "Musik ist der Schluessel zum Herzen." There was such a large German-American population in the city the paper didn't need to translate the phrase ("music is the key to the heart"). Later in the year, the *Beacon Journal* reminded Akronites to buy tickets for the upcoming season to support the club that had done a tremendous amount "for the good of Akron, and ... much to make Akron famous" (November 18, 1907).

In the early twentieth century, the club had two very distinct, but cooperative divisions—the study section, which required musical talent or intellect, and the chorus, which had a much larger membership. While the study section, chaired by Eva J. Heintselman—whose husband was the vice president of the Akron Extract and Chemical Company, which manufactured perfumes, flavoring extracts, and proprietary medicines—was the foundation of the club, the chorus brought the club fame, much to the delight of the club's honorary president Gertrude Seiberling. Her drive and determination was recognized as instrumental in bridging the gaps when the club faced dissolution, and her role would continue to expand locally and nationally.

As might be expected, Tuesday Musical's events were very genteel. While musical talent was the determining factor for membership, especially study section membership, the club was a gathering of Akron's socialites. A 1907 story about an afternoon recital described the scene in the following way:

> The affair was very pretty. Tea and sandwiches were served by white gowned girls from the daintily laid tea tables. The pourers were Mrs. R. M. Wannamaker and Mrs. Harry Hamlin. Mrs. Francis Seiberling and Mrs. Carrie Jacobs-Bond [the event's main performer] very informally received the members of the club and a few invited guests. (*Akron Beacon Journal*, October 30, 1907)

The growth of membership did bring up some issues that needed to be addressed, like the wearing of hats. During evening concerts, as a practice, ladies did not wear hats, but afternoon recitals brought out crowds in toques and much larger hats that could be as broad as the wearer's shoulders and adorned with masses of feathers and even stuffed hummingbirds. After complaints were raised about headgear blocking sight lines, the club requested that all ladies remove their hats for afternoon events.

The club continued to bring fine talent to the area, like Joseph L. Lhevinne, a famed Russian pianist. Lhevinne, whose "wide range of dynamics, an abundance of temperamental energy and a fine, massive touch," were coupled with the ability to render passages "as soft as silk" when demanded (*The Independent*, vol. 41, no. 2986, February 1906), was regarded as the best pianist from Russia since Anton Rubinstein. Support for the concert, in part, led to a year-end positive balance of $313.06, a result far better than in previous years. The club's treasurer, G. C. Donaldson, the manager of Pittsburgh Coal Company's Akron location, was confident in the club's progress. "If the Tuesday Musical Club continues the work that has been accomplished in the past two years, I see no reason why the club should not give just as good and even better concerts than ever before on its own merits without asking the public for money" (*Akron Beacon Journal*, June 3, 1907).

Under the presidency of Effie Bowman—who had replaced Ada B. House when she resigned for health reasons in 1908—Mademoiselle Schumann-Heink made a return visit to Akron; Mademoiselle Gerville-Reache, one of the world's greatest contraltos, appeared with violinist Leandro Campanari; and Reinald Werrenrath, America's most prominent baritone who would go on to become the musical director for NBC radio, sang for the club. Bowman was unable to continue her presidency in 1909 due to poor health and Fanny J. Wannamaker had to give up her position as the director of the afternoon section because she and her husband were moving to Cleveland. However, the season was a success because the club showed a positive financial balance after "thousands of dollars [were] taken in and thousands expended ... for expensive artists" (*Akron Beacon Journal*, April 25, 1909).

Katherine Bruot, who ran a local music studio, became president of the club and certainly had to feel good about the end-of-year balance of almost $600. In a step to encourage chorus membership, dues were reduced from five to two dollars because the club found that many citizens couldn't pay the higher fees. Gertrude Seiberling, the club's honorary president, continued to emphasize that Tuesday Musical's foundation and success were made possible by members joining together with a firm determination to carry out the club's mission.

Support for the club was becoming more visible. Prospects for the 1909–10 season looked bright. The *Akron Beacon Journal* listed the patrons for the club's concert series. Of course, the Seiberling family, company presidents, bankers, judges, doctors, and attorneys were represented, but so were stenographers and teachers. The most unique patron, though, had to be L. D. Triplett, whose occupation was listed as magnetic healer, a practice promoted throughout the country with sideshow-like events offering free entrance to anyone who was afflicted so that "the surest, quickest, and most reliable means of cure" (*Akron Daily Democrat*, June 7, 1899) could be offered to the suffering public.

The club could plan events with a better idea of revenue generation and had decided that a schedule of twelve afternoon recitals and three evening events made sense. While booking a series of important performers was always the club's intent, financial practices were also reviewed. In May 1911, the club had its books audited, reporting expenses of $5,534.53, which included amounts for a Steinway grand piano the club was paying off. The club offset these expenses with revenues of $6,184.53, leaving a balance of $650 to open the 1911–12 season (*Akron Beacon Journal*, May 17, 1911). Also, during the previous year, the enrollment of the study section had risen to ninety-three members "from the young girls just taking courage from the first fruits of successful study, to the mature woman whose many years of work in music have broadened her sympathy and appreciation for all lovers of art" (*Akron Beacon Journal*, November 28, 1910). Like the local economy, the club was growing.

Perpetuating the Music

IN 1912, TUESDAY MUSICAL Club celebrated its twenty-fifth anniversary. Many of the founding members had seen the club through tough times and were pleased that the enterprise was bringing culture to Akron. Gertrude Seiberling was forty-six years old and had become in many ways the spokesperson and public relations representative for the organization. Part of Gertrude Seiberling's love for singing that was "indescribably contagious" (*Akron Beacon Journal*, February 7, 1912) also drove her to ensure the club's success. After all, one skill she always emphasized was her ability to see an outcome that freed the club "from petty jealousies" (*Musical Monitor*, vol. 3, no. 6, 1913), allowing the organization to overcome obstacles and move forward.

At the 1911 season-ending banquet, Gertrude's husband, F. A.—who was always looking for productivity increases at his tire concern—indicated that Tuesday Musical might join up with the German club to form a large music organization to benefit from economies of scale and shared resources. While sentiment might have existed in favor of joining the two groups, though a past effort did not get very far, a Tuesday Musical member, Lina A. Rundell, seemed to voice the opinion of many of her compatriots—the club needed its own space and not one rented at the German-American Music Hall. The merger never took place. The German-American Society would continue to give its own concerts, but World War I and anti-German sentiment would lead to the society's demise in 1915.

Serendipity or not, Gertrude already had a plan for the club. In 1907, F. A. began purchasing farmland and cornfields north of downtown Akron in order to build a house for his family, which had outgrown their 158 East Market Street place. Gertrude took courses in architecture and design at Buchtel College, throwing herself into the new project like she did Tuesday Musical events. The Seiberlings held a design contest for the $150,000 home (which would ultimately cost $2 million) and Cleveland architect Charles S. Sumner won. A brilliant, eclectic architect, he had laid out the ornate Italian Renaissance-style Rockefeller physics building at Case Western's School of Applied Science and the office building of the Cleveland Baseball Company at League Park.

Gertrude's love for music was without question. F. A. was helping to make Akron America's boom town, but before he met Gertrude he had played the flute and was learning to play the cello. An invitation to President Taft's annual cabinet dinner at the request of Ohio Senator Charles Dick, who was from Akron and knew the couple well, not only showed how far Akron had come, but also provided a platform for Gertrude's talents. She performed in the East Room of the White House with Evan Williams and accompanist Katherine Bruot.

Both F. A. and Gertrude knew their country estate wouldn't be complete without a music room.

> Music has meant much in our home, and it has been the 'open sesame' to many doors of friendship and appreciation among the great and cultured. It has made life finer and more beautiful, the hard things of existence easier to bear, and interpreted the aspirations of the soul as no language or art can do. ... As for me, my life work is to broaden the opportunities for musical advancement in this community to the limit of my ability. It has grown much, but it is a constant warfare to keep commercialism from overwhelming other interests. (*Musical Monitor and World*, vol. 3, 1913, p. 172)

Gertrude was well aware of what the club needed. She was involved with the lecture-recital series at the club because this combination of performance and education expanded the knowledge of participants. The city also needed a larger auditorium for performers because the club was turning away around three hundred people who wanted tickets for fully-subscribed concerts. Even with the growing popularity of the club's offerings, Gertrude also pushed to establish an endowment fund to ensure long-term stability (*Musical Monitor and World*, vol. 3, 1913, pp. 171–72).

With finances not as much an issue, the club began to become more than an organization that sponsored afternoon lectures and evening concerts. It was becoming a part of the fabric of the city that was prospering as the rubber center of the country. Well-known artists were almost obliged to make Akron a stop on their performance circuits. Between 1910 and 1920, Tuesday Musical's slate of concerts featured:

- Kittie Cheatham, a renowned singer who specialized in performing African American folk songs;
- Cecil Fanning, a noted baritone known as the 'Poetsinger of Ohio;'
- John Barnes Wells, a tenor and composer of many light concert songs, including "Wishin' and Fishin'" and "Be the Best of Whatever You Are;"
- Alma Gluck, a member of the Metropolitan Opera and as popular as Ernestine Schumann-Heink;
- Ernest Schelling, a famed pianist and composer who made his first public appearance at the age of four;
- Margarete Matzenauer, the Hungarian-born mezzo-soprano of the Metropolitan Opera;
- Ignace Paderewski, called the greatest Polish pianist of his time, who would go on to become the second prime minster of the Second Republic of Poland;
- Ethel Leginska a pianist of great distinction, dubbed by the *New York Herald Tribune* "the Paderewski of women pianists," and a pioneering conductor and composer.

Tuesday Musical sponsored performances of *La Bohème*, *Carmen*, and Handel's *Messiah*, and brought in the Philadelphia Symphony and the Cincinnati Orchestra. In 1918, the club invited the Cleveland Orchestra, which was founded in the same year, to perform for the Akron subscribers. (With the exception of one year, the Cleveland Orchestra has played in Akron annually.)

The lecture-recital series brought music knowledge about various topics. Howard Brockway, who would become a faculty member at the Julliard School of Music, gave a talk on operas. Thomas Whitney Surette, the author of *Course of Study on the Development of Symphonic Music,* addressed the club. Members heard talks on the operas *Tiefland* by Eugene d'Albert and *Mona* by Horatio Parker, the latter prior to its premier at the Metropolitan Opera.

Tuesday Musical reached out to audiences who would be unlikely to pay for and enjoy evening events. Newsboys were invited to a free concert in 1912 that featured the contributions of local performers. The *Akron Beacon Journal* slyly noted, "The newsboys are a critical audience, but the club members held their attention." And why not? The program had closed with the singing of "America," a vote of thanks by the audience, and "three rousing cheers" (November 20, 1912).

Gertrude Seiberling likely prompted the club to schedule events to provide aid to society's less fortunate. After all, part of her husband's initiatives included building model communities, like Goodyear Heights and Fairlawn Heights, which featured single-family homes, schools, and parks for rubber workers. F. A. Seiberling also funded events for his employees, like the second annual Goodyear Field Day of 1917, which brought fifty thousand workers, and their families and friends together to find "Something Doing Every Minute."

> The day's program was topped off with a spectacular flight of one of the Goodyear dirigibles. The giant airship propelled itself gracefully over the field in a series of figure eights, at an altitude of about 500 feet, and dropped paper bombs on the crowd below. Many of these "bombs" contained valuable prizes and were scrambled for with enthusiasm by thousands of persons. (*Automobile Trade Journal*, October 1917, p. 132)

As part of its activities, the club wanted to sponsor a Children's Crusade in 1917. The event would involve a chorus of three hundred Akron school children who would take part in the program, accompanied by a symphony orchestra, as the last concert of the season. The number of participants would necessitate the use of the new armory building, which was to be completed by the May concert date. Unfortunately, the concert was cancelled because the armory's opening was delayed.

A child did play, literally, into the club plans the following year when Reginald Riley performed at a Tuesday Musical concert. Riley, a homegrown piano prodigy, studied under the direction of Rena Wills, a local music teacher and most likely a club member. At a Tuesday Musical-sponsored concert, the twelve-year-old played Mendelssohn's Rondo Capriccioso from memory and finished off his performance with Brahms' Seventh Hungarian Dance. Riley later was the preeminent pianist at the American Federation of Music's National American Musical Festival in Buffalo, New York, in 1922. His career never led to tremendous national acclaim, but he continued to be a part of Tuesday Musical concerts for several years.

Ella C. Bigelow, Tuesday Musical president in 1917, was probably relieved and enthused about the November completion of the Akron Armory. The planning and construction of the building had dragged on, at times delayed by supplies and materials needed for the war effort. The armory, the most artistic the state had constructed, was designed to accommodate three companies of infantry and a regimental band. The main feature of the space was a combination drill hall and auditorium that could accommodate three thousand people. The building cost a little over $165,000 of which $50,000 was donated by the citizens of Akron (*Ohio General Statistics*, vol. 5, Harvey C. Smith, Secretary of State, 1919).

Befitting Akron's new found prosperity, the armory's opening was coupled with an auto show where fifty-eight makes of cars would be on display. Ohio's Governor, James Cox, Akron's Mayor, W. J. Laub, prominent Akron citizens, and officer from Camps Sherman and Columbus gave speeches during the dedication. Undoubtedly, many Tuesday Musical members and their husbands attended the gala night activities on December 1, 1917, since the celebration was aimed at Akron's upper crust, especially the rubber barons.

The philanthropic activities of the club were in evidence at a community Christmas concert held at the new armory on December 23.

The concert, likely the first held in the space by the club, raised an estimated $500 for Akron's less-fortunate, allowing them to enjoy a happy holiday. Many club regulars, including Gertrude Seiberling, Mabel Motz, and Adeline Voss-Eichelberger gave performances.

The longer-standing club ladies performed with a heavy heart. Earlier that month, Helen Storer Collins, who had been seriously ill, passed away in Cleveland. Collins, who had roomed with Mina Miller (the future Mrs. Thomas Edison) at Wellesley College, provided a great deal of direction during the club's early existence.

When the new year started, an *Akron Beacon Journal* article seemed to strain the relationship between Tuesday Musical and the newspaper. For over a decade, the paper had been a strong supporter of the club, probably because the editor's wife, Clara I. Knight was a strong backer of the arts in Akron and especially Tuesday Musical. The 1918 dispute arose around a review in the paper that was critical of Ethel Leginska's performance. The reviewer, using only his initials "K. N." (as in know nothing), poked fun at:

- Leginska's agent (whose duty was to "compose new combinations of adjectives, adverbs, and nouns descriptive of his boss");
- Leginska herself (Leginska couldn't be "her real name for she has quite a distinctive Irish face");
- The audience ("One old man calmly read a magazine while she played");
- And classical music (Leginska would have been better received if she had played "Annie Laurie," "Last Rose of Summer," and "When You and I Were Young, Maggie," all folk tunes). (*Akron Beacon Journal*, February 20, 1918)

The club's ladies would have none of the tongue-in-cheek criticism of the most accomplished female pianist of the time. True, Leginska could be temperamental and was described as being a bit weird. True, a *New York Times* article a few years earlier indicated that she was not at her best during one of her classical performances at Carnegie Hall (November 3, 1916). True, she was going through a messy divorce, and even though she was of English ancestry, her last name led some people to believe that she was Russian in an era of anti-Russian feelings stemming from World War I. However, as Ella Bigelow put it in a strongly worded letter to the editor, "The large audience that braved the storm last Tuesday evening to hear Mme. Leginska certainly approved in the most enthusiastic manner ... When everybody in Akron acquires the habit of attending the club concerts (now that we have the armory with large seating capacity) our city will become more musical every year and realize that 'America needs your voice for it is the voice of courage'" (*Akron Beacon Journal*, February 22, 1918). While it would be a big leap to consider the entire affair a public relations opportunity, calling on Akronites to support Tuesday Musical concerts in a show of patriotism might have been the end in mind.

The club finished its season at the armory and elected a new president for the evening section; Adeline Voss-Eichelberger would succeed Ella Bigelow, who had overseen the two most successful years of the club's growth (*Akron Beacon Journal*, March 12, 1918). Voss-Eichelberger's background included touring the greater Akron area as part of the Mendelssohn Quartette along with her husband T. S. Eichelberger (tenor), Florence H. Phelps (contralto), and F. W. Work (baritone). The quartette was accompanied by Clara Collins.

By the time the club had elected its new officers, the United States had been involved in World War I for a little over a year. Gertrude Seiberling had watched as one of her sons, John Frederick, paraded off to El Paso, Texas for training. He was a first lieutenant in the army during the conflict. Ohioans would suffer during the War, with over sixteen thousand casualties and over four thousand deaths. Those numbers seem large, but pale in comparison to an epidemic that struck the globe during the fall of 1918.

Akronite Clarence Hicks was a twenty-four-year-old delivery driver for the Akron Dry Goods Company. His rounds might have taken him to any number of Tuesday Musical members' houses. On the weekend of October 26, 1918, Hicks was one of six people who succumbed to Spanish Influenza, a pandemic that would kill an estimated fifty million people worldwide.

By November, Akron had experienced 242 deaths and almost three thousand additional reported cases. Public meetings were cancelled. Goodyear called off its training schools and halted foremen or worker gatherings. Colleges closed their doors and sent students home. Theaters and football fields were shuttered. Tuesday Musical couldn't use the armory for any concerts, even if it wanted to do so, because the building had become a makeshift hospital to treat the stricken.

While concerts were out of the question, the club continued to impact the Akron music scene. In October, Tuesday Musical, under the auspices of the Akron Music League, brought in Earl C. Killeen to direct the choruses and community singers citywide. The Akron Music League was created "to work with existing musical organizations, to back the community singing work, to organize the annual evening concerts, at which the artists of national reputation are brought to Akron and to build up a great Akron orchestra" (*Akron Beacon Journal*, September 18, 1919). Many of Tuesday Musical members, including Gertrude Seiberling, Clara Collins, and Adeline Voss-Eichelberger played a part in the league's operation and activities, and the participation made sense. The league was funded in the amount of $25,000 by an outgrowth of Akron's War Chest—the Better Akron Federation, an organization that was providing funds to seventeen philanthropic and educational organizations, including the YMCA, the People's Hospital, the Salvation Army, the Boy and Girl Scouts, and the Catholic Service League.

The music league, however, was top-heavy with male leadership, an issue that had to cause some concern with the Tuesday Musical ladies. For over three decades, Tuesday Musical had experienced the rise and fall of music interest in Akron and had been able to survive and flourish. Nonetheless, the additional capital might allow the club to defray costs.

In the postwar recession period, Killeen, who had also taken on the role of the league's manager, faced the reality of an era of diminishing funds. The federation was only able to provide the league $10,000 and other amounts would have to come from the league's directors and the general public. Economic conditions had restricted charitable giving, which ultimately forced the league to dissolve.

As the ravages of the Spanish Influenza began to diminish, Akron and the rest of the country received the news in early November that an armistice had been signed by Germany, ending the Great War. Wild celebrations ensued all over town "that eclipsed any public demonstration ever witnessed in the city. ... Employees of all rubber factories and machine shops left their work on hearing the news ... A parade headed by Sheriff James Corey, Judge William Ahern of the common pleas court and an impromptu band was a nucleus for the celebration. ... All clerical work in ... city hall was suspended ... Letter carriers and postoffice workers were given a half-holiday" (*Cleveland Plain Dealer*, November 8, 1919).

One music dealer saw a greater opportunity for the general appreciation of music with the war's end.

> While music during the war was recognized as a most vital and useful factor, and was encouraged to a remarkable degree, it was, nevertheless, used somewhat as we use any instrument, as a means to an end. The thought of music for music's sake was held in abeyance. This condition or state of mind is now happily changed. Music may now present its claim as a fine art without the fear of running counter to the idea of patriotism, and all lovers of music can proceed to enjoy music to the full for its own sake.
>
> Likewise they can discuss it as an art—an art sufficient in itself and justifying its own existence—and they need not now speak of it merely as a vehicle for the emotional display of patriotism.
>
> Just as music has helped patriotism, so patriotism has helped music. Patriotism has given music a substantial foundation on which to stand. Music has labored under the handicap that many good people considered it merely as an emotion, and that to indulge freely in the delight of music spelled the yielding too much to emotionalism.
>
> The war showed the fallacy of this reasoning. It showed that music is woven in the woof and warp of humanity; that it is a part of and strengthens the sterner virtues; that it not only idealizes and inspires, but that it re-enforces the character and the resolution for the accomplishment of hard duties and stern tasks. (*The Music Trades*, vol. 56, no. 21, 1918)

The last year of the decade, 1919, brought a sense of normalcy back to Tuesday Musical. The evening concerts were held again, officers were elected, and the study section could hold afternoon meetings to discuss musical topics and hear recitals. The country may have gone dry, but music in Akron was flowing.

Leading the Nation

AS AMERICA ENTERED THE Roaring Twenties, a new technology was threatening live music performances—radio. Alma Gluck, who had performed for Tuesday Musical, didn't see a place for broadcasts in her future. "I think that radio is here to stay ... but I do not see how an established artist can ever afford to sing for it. Possibly beginners who might be glad to accept $5,000 or $10,000 a year to sing exclusively for the radio, would find it profitable ... but I do think that they [producers] are looking in the wrong direction when they come to the established artists, the phonograph artists, and ask them to broadcast." When she was to perform at an Oklahoma City concert, she arrived to find that ticket sales were nonexistent. Asking around, she found that in order to publicize her concert, the backers had broadcast her songs on the radio (*The Wireless Age*, vol. 10, no. 10, July 1923).

The impact of radio was mild compared to the post-World War I depression of 1920–21 that impacted the country's economy. Many experts consider the economic downturn as severe as the Great Depression, but it is not as well-known because the economy recovered quickly. However, during the upheaval, production dropped by one-third and wholesale prices fell by 50 percent. During the last year of the war, unemployment was at 1.4 percent. In 1921, at the height of the depression, unemployment reached almost 12 percent. In May 1921, Akron reported unemployment of twenty thousand; an increase from twelve thousand in March of that year (*New York Times*, May 21, 1921). A year previously, Akron had reported a shortage of 1,000 workers (*New York Times*, February 9, 1920).

With economic woes facing the country, Gertrude Seiberling became the ninth president of the National Federation of Music Clubs. Her three-year term started in 1919 and saw member clubs grow from four hundred to a thousand. She also started a new department—the Junior Department—which was quite in line with her interest in creating opportunities for children to become acquainted with the cultural value of classical music. She was afraid that contemporary music was only a means to supply "jazz dancing tunes so the young people would be content to stay at home ... turn back the rug, and spend an hour or two fox-trotting" (*Journal of the Proceedings of the Fourteenth Annual Meeting of Music Supervisors' National Conference*, 1921, pp. 207–8). In a speech given at the Music Supervisors' National Conference that was held in St. Joseph, Missouri, from April 4–8, 1921, Seiberling reiterated the club's working slogan: "A music club in every town, in every county, in every state of the Union, and junior boys and girls clubs auxiliary" (*Journal of the Proceedings of the Fourteenth Annual Meeting of Music Supervisors' National Conference*, 1921, p. 210).

Being away from Akron might have been a respite for Gertrude. Her husband was trying to keep Goodyear afloat; the company was financially overextended and in danger of going bankrupt. In May, on Friday the 13th, F. A. Seiberling was ousted as the president of the company under a financial arrangement that kept the company solvent. At the time of the transition, he had total liabilities of almost $7 million, but his creditors granted him a settlement extension. In all likelihood, Seiberling could have met his obligations if he sold Stan Hywet. Rather than do so, he put the property in his wife's name (*Automotive Industries*, vol. 44, no. 25, June 23, 1921).

He summed up the refinancing action and its necessity quite eruditely.

> The nation-wide slump in business last fall brought our business to the verge of disaster. Since that hour I have had but one purpose, to save this business from a receivership and this community from the results of such a calamity. That was accomplished yesterday and the new management inherits a business soundly financed. ... there is no

> reason why Goodyear cannot move forward to a higher plane than it has yet achieved. (*Motor Age*, vol. 39, no. 20, May 19, 1921)

Within the year, F. A. Seiberling would begin his own tire label, Seiberling Tire, with plants in Barberton, Ohio, and New Castle, Pennsylvania. By the end of the 1930s, he brokered his Goodyear stock, equity he retained as part of the transition arrangement, for a substantial profit.

Tuesday Musical weathered the financial storm and seemed to improve its community status. At the year-end meeting in May 1921, the club reported a positive balance of $2,000 and expressed gratitude for the work the club had accomplished under the leadership of Effie Bowman, which included organizing "an artist course of concerts in Goodyear theater; organizing several junior and one senior club auxiliary; presenting concerts at various institutions through the Altruistic department; providing teachers for more than thirty little folks of the Children's home; [and] promoting a music memory contest in the public schools" (*Akron Beacon Journal*, May 18, 1921).

Vernie G. Kimball wrote a toast to the club that was sung at the event by Ruth F. Mather, the afternoon chairperson.

> There are reasons we should love it. Need I tell you?
> And reasons we should praise it in song and story, too;
> 'Tis because it's [sic] aim and purpose is so noble, high and true.
> Always to the best aspiring, serving too.
>
> These are the reasons I would toast it in song to you,
> Quite mindful of its present, past and future, too.
> May advancement mark its future, may it rise to be the hub
> In Our City's Wheel of Progress, Tuesday Musical Club. (*Akron Beacon Journal*, May 18, 1921)

The poor economic situation did force the club to discontinue its evening concert series the following year, but not its community work. The junior club emphasis was evident in the number of such entities that had been formed, including Akron's own St. Cecilia Choral

Club, an organization of thirty voices. Tuesday Musical had also been instrumental in creating six other junior auxiliaries: the Evan Williams, the Mayflower, the Pilgrim, the McDowell, the Chopin, and the Beethoven. Members of the club could be found performing weekly at the infirmary, the Children's Home, the sanatorium, or the Sumner House for the Aged.

At the suggestion of Gertrude Seiberling, the club brought classical music to local schoolchildren by way of the Musical Memory Contest. The 1921 event was the "biggest undertaking ever attempted in the Akron public schools, with 30,000 competing in the elimination contests" (*Music Trade Review*, May 7, 1921). The finals were held in the Akron Armory on April 29, when student teams from twenty-eight Akron schools competed. Their task was to identify the title, composer, and composer's nationality of the twenty selections played by an orchestra. The Robinson School team won with a perfect score; the Portage Path and Lincoln Schools tied for second and the Miller School took third place.

Chalmers K. Stewart recalled the contest. In 1918, after his family moved to Akron from Milwaukee to be a part of the burgeoning tire industry, he attended Henry Elementary School located on the corner of Forge and Arch Streets. Stewart would eventually become an English teacher.

> Every year a music memory contest was held. This consisted of, I think, a hundred records of classical music, snippets of which had to be identified. You won a gold, silver, or bronze medallion, depending on how well you did. It was mostly the girls, wearers of hair ribbons and otherwise torchbearers of culture as well, who participated. Once, the music teachers, hoping to sandbag one of us innocents, slipped a ringer on the victorola, a record not on the list. Sure enough, up shot Max Griffen's hand. "That's 'Traumerei,'" he said; and so it was. That's what came of taking private violin lessons. (*Memories of the Akron Public Schools,* Akron Public Schools, July 1999)

The years from 1921 until at least 1945 can surely be regarded as the Bowman era of Tuesday Musical. Effie Bowman was the wife of physician and surgeon D. S. Bowman and lived on Crosby Street from about 1900, though her family changed addresses a few times, beginning at 151 Crosby and continuing to 345 Crosby. Effie Bowman had grown up in McConnelsville, Ohio (about thirty miles south of Zanesville, Ohio), and she and her husband had spent some time in Homeworth, Ohio (south of Alliance, Ohio).

In many ways, Effie Bowman was the opposite of Gertrude Seiberling. Seiberling was very comfortable on the national stage and loved to tell people about the cultural value of music appreciation. Bowman embodied quiet leadership, coupled with a knack for business and organizational acumen. She was able to keep Tuesday Musical profitable and bring in artists of national and international quality. In 1925, she tried to resign as club president due to poor health, but the members delayed naming a successor until she returned from a recuperative trip. They wanted her to continue because the club had "enjoyed greater success during Mrs. Bowman's regime than at any other period of its history" (*Akron Beacon Journal*, May 26, 1925). Considering the times in which she served, her management is remarkable because the country went through two depressions, including the collapse of the United States' financial system in 1929.

Bowman's influence extended outside of Akron, having had a large role in the development of Helen Jepson's career. Jepson, a soprano who sang at the Metropolitan Opera and with other American companies in the 1930s and 1940s, grew up in Akron and would perform for Tuesday Musical on several occasions, including at the inaugural event of the club's fiftieth season. Bowman's and Jepson's paths crossed when Jepson was a young singer and Bowman was the choir leader at the Woodland Methodist Episcopal Church. Bowman was impressed with Jepson's voice and began singing her praises around the city. Eventually, Gertrude Seiberling was introduced to Jepson, and along with Bowman, provided the means to support the protégé's musical education (*Cleveland Plain Dealer*, April 15, 1937).

Effie Bowman's interest in developing future talent led her to organize an 'opera laboratory' in October 1930. The school was aimed at all "professional and amateur singers, vocal teachers, choir leaders, choral directors and others interested in studying grand opera, particularly persons of other nationality living in and near Akron" (*Cleveland Plain Dealer*, October 17, 1930). The 'laboratory' was based on plans used by local opera groups in Europe and the club hoped to stage local performances with those trained in the school, furthering the development of operatic talent, an initiative that other American cities had undertaken. The musical director for the opera group was Francesco de Leone, who founded the music department at the (Municipal) University of Akron.

Women in Music History

1924: Elisabeth Kuyper founds the American Women's Symphony Orchestra in New York City.

1933: Florence Price's Piano Concerto is performed by the Chicago Symphony, marking the first time an African American woman's composition is performed by a major symphony.

1944: The premier of Martha Graham's ballet *Appalachian Spring*, to music composed by Aaron Copland, takes place.

Reaching into the community during the twenties to educate children, teenagers, and adults about classical music has to be viewed as a reaction in some ways to the Charleston, the cake walk, the black bottom, the flea hop, and other motifs of the Roaring Twenties. The ladies of Tuesday Musical could hardly be identified as flappers and were determined to rally against the modernity of jazz and the likes of Paul Whiteman, the 'King of Jazz.' Perhaps, some of the ladies held the sentiment of Emile Gilmer, who headed London's Civic Band. Gilmer intended to bring his musicians to America and "take jazz to bits before the public's eye and expose its fallacy, and show the public how it is constructed and scored, compared to real music" (*Cleveland Plain Dealer*, December 18, 1927).

Still, Tuesday Musical did sponsor National Music Week, an event created by the National Bureau for the Advancement of Music—an organization established in 1916 by the National Piano Manufacturers Association to heighten the public's interest in all types of composition, and of course, to sell pianos. In 1924, the National Federation of Music Clubs supported the Music Week program (which it still supports today). The founder of the concept, C. M. Tremaine, who had been the vice president of the Aeolian Company (Stan Hywet Hall has an Aeolian organ), a manufacturer of player organs and pianos, described the event as a suggestion,

> as contrasted with a super imposed project, and its spread has been due far more to public responsiveness to the idea than to any campaign. Getting people to do something you wish them to do and think they should do is vastly different from suggesting their doing something they will want to do and which will bring them enjoyment and refreshing recreation. The latter conception is the basis on which Music Week rests, and accounts for its remarkable growth. (C. M. Tremaine, *History of National Music Week*, New York: National Bureau for the Advancement of Music, 1925)

Emma H. Shreffler, whose husband was the treasurer of the Lyman-Hawkins Lumber Company, was in charge of the committee that planned a citywide celebration for Music Week with the cooperation of theaters, schools, clubs, stores, the public library, and WADC, a local radio station. The emphasis was on music in daily life. The week of activities was kicked off by Vincent Stevens, the secretary of the Chamber of Commerce, who gave a Sunday night speech on WADC.

In 1926, in tune with giving back to the community, Tuesday Musical (at the suggestion of Effie Bowman) took steps to help those who couldn't afford the regular cost of a season subscription. Aimed at students and blue-collar workers, the club reserved a section of about a hundred seats to be sold at a nominal charge of $1.50 each (about $18.50 in 2013). The club already gave free musical programs once or twice a month at the Strand Theater on Main Street and the ladies of the club also gave free organ recitals at various churches throughout the area. As Bowman put it, "the community has grown both in population and ideals and there are more ways for advancing the love of music today than there were then [1887]" (*Akron Beacon Journal*, March 24, 1926).

The Roaring Twenties ended with the stock market crash of October 29, 1929. Until the United States went to war in late 1941, unemployment ranged from around 9 percent to a high of almost 25 percent. From 1932 until 1935, unemployment was over 20 percent (Bureau of Labor Statistics). A family of four that was earning $2,400 in 1929 "had to get by on $1,200 in 1932, provided it was getting by at all" (Vincent Curcio, *Chrysler: The Life and Times of Automotive Genius*, New York: Oxford University Press, 2000, p. 491).

Since Akron was tied closely with the auto industry, when car sales fell by 75 percent from 1929 to 1933, (Robert Asher and Ronald Edford, eds., *Autowork*, Albany: SUNY University Press, 1995, p. 73), the city's tire workers suffered greatly and labor unrest was prevalent. By 1933, more than 40 percent of Ohio factory workers and 67 percent of Ohio construction workers were unemployed. In 1932, Ohio's unemployment rate for all residents reached 37.3 percent (Ohio History Central).

One factor that kept Akron's tire manufacturers in better shape than those located elsewhere was the higher concentration of manufacturing in Akron, allowing for economies of scale that enabled companies like Goodyear and Firestone to ride out periods of low demand. It wasn't until the end of the decade that Akron's tire firms sought other manufacturing locations—due, in part, to unionization—and tire manufacturing concentration declined in the city. In 1929, tire concerns employed 53,172 workers; by 1939 the number had dropped to 30,579 (Ralph W. Frank, "Decentralization of the Akron Rubber Industry," *The Ohio Journal of Science*, vol. 61, no. 1, January 1961). Even though manufacturing declined, executive positions remained, creating a stratum of residents who could contribute to the area's cultural activities.

During the 1930s, Tuesday Musical would celebrate its fiftieth anniversary, and from all indications, the club's concert series and other activities continued during the era of long breadlines and transients riding the country's rails in search of jobs. Akron was kind to nonfamily males looking for employment by providing them with meals, but in the end, instructing them to move on. Akron's fine music lovers were kind to the club, too, buying subscriptions to ensure that famed artists would be on stage each season. The prominent performers were a who's who of the music scene:

- 1930—Lawrence Tibbett, baritone of the Metropolitan Opera
- 1931—Helen Jepson, soprano of the Metropolitan Opera
- 1932—José Iturbi, Spanish pianist, compared to Vladimir Horowitz
- 1933—Fritz Kreisler, world-famous violinist
- 1934—Maria Olszewska, contralto of the Metropolitan Opera
- 1935—Helen Jepson
- 1936—Orpheus Male Chorus
- 1937—Jooss European Ballet, noted for their works of compassion and social consequence, including "The Green Table"
- 1938—Poldi Mildner, a twenty-two-year-old Viennese pianist
- 1939—Grace Moore, celebrated soprano

Celebrated during its 1937–38 season, the fiftieth anniversary of the club brought together an extra-special program of performers, including Jepson, the Vienna Boys Choir, the Jooss Ballet, Rose Bampton (a Metropolitan Opera star, born in 1907 in Lakewood, Ohio), Iso Briselli (a Russian violinist), Tibbett, Mildner, and the Cleveland Orchestra, under the direction of Artur Rodzinski. In addition, the club sponsored a series of three chamber music concerts, managed by Gertrude Seiberling, with a series price of five dollars.

An unfortunate occurrence during the golden anniversary of the club ultimately provided a benefit that augmented and strengthened the finances of the organization. Mary E. Schumacher—longtime club supporter and second wife of Akron's Oatmeal King, Ferdinand Schumacher—left $50,000 (about $806,000 in 2013) to the club for concerts. Eventually, this amount, through further investments, would quadruple in value. Mary Schumacher travelled extensively before her death and was always on the lookout for talent that Tuesday Musical could showcase. On one trip to Hawaii, she actually helped set up a Tuesday Musical Club there.

Mary Schumacher's gift came almost fifty years after a rebirth of Schumacher's oats empire. An 1886 fire had destroyed the factory of the uninsured businessman, saddling him with a loss of $600,000. Undaunted, he proposed a merger with the Akron Milling Company to create the F. Schumacher Milling Company. Part of the ability to create a new enterprise hinged on the preference of consumers for Schumacher's product—it tasted better. Eventually, Schumacher would face several financial setbacks, but the estate he left his wife and her subsequent gift to Tuesday Musical ensured decades of concerts for Akron's population and provided funds for the club's initial scholarship programs.

In 1939, the New York World's Fair was underway, guided by the theme: "Building the World of Tomorrow with the Tools of Today." The official fair song, composed by the late George Gershwin, sounded a hopeful cry after a decade of despair for many Americans.

> Sound the brass, roll the drum
> To the world of tomorrow we come
> See the sun through the grey
> It's the dawn of a new day
> ...
> Tell the world at the door
> That we don't want him around anymore
> Better times are here to stay
> As we live and laugh the American way
> (Ira Gershwin and George Gershwin, Ira Gershwin Music/George Gershwin Music/WB Music Corp.)

For Akronites, even though there had to be some apprehension over events taking place in Europe, the worst of the Depression seemed over. Even more heartening for Tuesday Musical was the realization that subscribers were willingly supporting its concert series. The club had built a very dynamic organizational structure and understood their finances fully. They had succeeded in building a movement that was embedded into Akron's annual cycle of events. Tuesday Musical was committed as ever to encouraging the musical appreciation of tomorrow with the hard work and determination of the present.

The End of an Era

TUESDAY MUSICAL'S 1941–42 SEASON program included a scheduled late November appearance by Rose Bampton, the Metropolitan Opera star who was a Lakewood, Ohio, native. Bampton would live for almost a century, dying at the age of ninety-nine in August 2007. Along with the Met star, her brother and sister-in-law Mr. and Mrs. James Bampton were to come to the city as guests of Jean Bowman. If all went well, Bampton's husband Wilfred Pelletier, one of the Met's top-ranked conductors, would also attend. Stan Hywet was to be the site of an after-concert party, since the Bamptons would be the Seiberling's house guests.

The concert scheduled for the Akron Armory never took place. Bampton became ill during an earlier Chicago appearance. She contacted a personal friend, Marguerite Sorg of Massillon, a local choirmaster and performer, to let her know that she had to return to New York to recuperate.

Less than two weeks later, Pearl Harbor was attacked and the lives of Americans were changed drastically. At the time, Akron had five tire manufacturers: Goodyear, Goodrich, Firestone, General, and Mohawk; and the Seiberling Company was producing rubber products in nearby Barberton. The war depleted the Akron area of the vast majority of its factory workers, necessitating the employment of older Americans, high school boys, housewives, and young women. Rosie the Riveter became the symbol of industries that had to expand production to supply the booming war effort.

Women working for a purpose had been routine for the ladies of Tuesday Musical. Effie Bowman, in her seventies, was still the stable factor in organizing the club's activities at the outbreak of the war. She would finally give up the reigns in 1945. Gertrude Seiberling, also in her seventies, the visible face of the club, was beginning to scale back her participation. Both, however, had built an organization that could sustain itself.

During the war, the ladies of the club had to make adjustments due to government rationing of sugar, coffee, meat, butter, tires, and gasoline. Instead of being able to drive to Stan Hywet for their annual campaign meetings, some ladies arrived on bicycles. Catered events turned into picnic-style, bring-your-own-dish affairs. The quality of concerts did not decline under war conditions. The Cleveland Orchestra kept up its annual visits to Akron; Helen Jepson returned to supportive audiences; the famed violinist Yehudi Menuhin took the stage at the armory; the twenty-two-year-old American pianist phenom William Kapell was booked; and the club even had a concert entitled "Opera for Everyone" to broaden its subscriber base.

War production was a boon for Akron-area workers. During World War II, the Goodyear Aircraft Corporation (GAC) manufactured 104 airships for the military at its Akron facility. The firm also built F4U Corsair planes for the United States Navy. When Goodyear created GAC in 1939, this branch of the company employed just thirty workers. By 1942, GAC consisted of thirty-five thousand employees (Ohio History Central). Other area firms experienced similar spikes in manufacturing. The strata of Akron's society who frequented Tuesday Musical events were in the position to continue their attendance during the war.

On September 2, 1945, the Japanese formally surrendered, ending World War II. The mothers and fathers of Akron whose sons had survived the ordeal awaited their homecomings. Perhaps the country could rediscover a semblance of normalcy, though the adjustment might take years.

By late 1945, Effie Bowman and Gertrude Seiberling had seen the evolution of Akron from horses to bikes to cars. They had watched fortunes grow through the development of the rubber industry. They had heard the stories of Civil War veterans, the tales of World War I doughboys, and the anecdotes of World War II soldiers. Both ladies had listened to the strains of countless opera stars, the symphonic music of world-class orchestras, and the melodies of dynamic baritones. The women were bound together in bringing culture to Northeast Ohio. Their substantial lives also ended within weeks of each other; on December 14, 1945, Effie Bowman passed away and Gertrude Seiberling died in her sleep on January 8, 1946.

By column inch or any other measure, Gertrude Seiberling's death received greater coverage. Her obituary even appeared in the *New York Times*. At eighty, her death was a shock because Gertrude Seiberling was still active, having strolled in the spring-like weather only days before her death. The *Akron Beacon Journal* indicated that "[o]ne could not mention music in Akron without also mentioning the name of Mrs. Seiberling" (January 8, 1946) because she was "a pioneer in bringing music to a city devoted to the smoke and roar of industry" (January 9, 1946). Her accomplishments and contributions would find a lasting place in Akron's history. Akron music lovers, though, would have to adjust to armory concerts without the presence of "Mrs. Seiberling in that chair near the front and to the left" (*Akron Beacon Journal*, January 9, 1946). On January 29, the Cleveland Orchestra included in its Tuesday Musical program Schubert's "Unfinished Symphony" in her memory.

The announcement of Effie Bowman's death was a scant three paragraphs. She died after a long illness on a day when Akron experienced a massive snow storm, snarling rush hour traffic. The city was in the midst of a cold spell, sending temperatures into the single digits. Her funeral services were held at the Woodland M.E. Church, and she was buried in Rose Hill Park. The paper noted that she "was very active in Akron music circles ... and belonged to several national music organizations" (*Akron Beacon Journal*, December 15, 1945). Bowman's passing went almost as unnoticed as her role in leading Tuesday Musical through tough American economic times (and her contributions have never before been fully recognized).

The deaths of the club's honorary president and of the president who oversaw operations for almost one-quarter century also coincided in many ways with the end of an era in American music and culture.

When Tuesday Musical was founded, every respectable household had a piano and families and friends gathered to sing along to new sheet music (James F. Richardson, "Vocal Recitals in Smaller Cities: Changes in Supply, Demand and Content since the 1920s," *Journal of Cultural Economics*, vol. 5, no. 1, 1981, pp. 21–35). As part of this tradition, recital audiences expected performers to include some popular material in their productions, and they were willing to subscribe to Tuesday Musical's balanced programs, which had something for everyone. The advent of new forms of music and expanded media outlets impacted listening audiences. The club's offerings would be viewed more and more as music for the elite class as newer generations began to rock 'n' roll. The path to this bifurcation was evident in a 1956 lieder recital by soprano Irmgard Seefried and Paul Ulanowsky. Half the audience left at intermission, not thrilled with a concert of all German-language songs. By the next decade, programs almost entirely in languages other than English were the norm (Richardson, 1981, pp. 21–35). This reality had a great impact on prospective members.

Tuesday Musical's aim to bring world-renowned artists to Akron did not change substantially. The club, however, would have to rethink how best to fulfill its purpose and modify and enhance its strategies. In the post-Bowman era, Tuesday Musical presidents would have to rely on their experiences and the ideas of club members to design new methods to keep the club moving forward. Unfortunately, in the early 1950s, Club Historian Louise Harper had to inform the members of the club that the past might not prove to be a guide to the future.

> I am sorry this report must be written. ... Soon after our club was founded in 1887 a scrapbook was started, containing pictures and items of interest to the young group. When filled, another was added, and another, up to the present time—with the exception of the current one, dated 1943–1953, these books have all disappeared—no one seems to know where. (Historian Report 1951–1952, Tuesday Musical Collection, University of Akron Archives)

Long-standing club members obviously provided a link to the past, but new initiatives were advanced to enhance the club's mission of fostering classical music. One area that saw rapid development was Tuesday Musical's scholarship program. In 1953, four club members—Betty Dornan, Lydia Colopy, Kathryn Browning, and Ellen Herberich, who would go on to become the scholarship chairperson—met to discuss the possibility of giving scholarships to students majoring in music. By 1957, the club was awarding Tuesday Musical Club Memorial scholarships to four individuals who were twenty-five years old or younger and had "outstanding musical ability" (Scholarship Brochure, Tuesday Musical Collection, University of Akron Archives). One scholarship was for piano (the Mary Schumacher scholarship); one was for voice (the Gertrude and Frank Seiberling scholarship); one was for organ; and the other was for an orchestral instrument. The club also set up a University of Akron scholarship, which was awarded to a full-time student who showed promise in the field of applied music.

To continue to impact the lives of young women interested in music, the club also set up the Martha App Scholarship Loan. Martha App had been a club member since her student days. The loan was given to an aspiring artist from Summit County and had a few unique stipulations. The loan could be repaid within five years without interest. Further, the loan was to be repaid before the recipient's marriage. Perhaps the club ladies thought the requirements would allow the recipient to be more active in the club after graduating.

Over the years, the scholarships kept growing due to the generosity of donors. Names like Winifred Collins, Mary Louise Irvin, John Charles Frentz, Zada Willaman, Gertrude Pflaum, Ruby Bird, and many others were added to scholarships awarded to promising musicians of voice, piano, strings, woodwind, and brass. The club's scholarship fund, after all, wasn't insignificant, amounting to over $125,000 by the late 1990s.

The club's consistent scheduling of world-famous acts at affordable prices has had lasting and, at times, unexpected results. Arden Yockey began his teaching career as a music instructor in the Conesville, Ohio, schools in the late 1930s. He was elected president of the Coshocton County Music Educators organization in 1937. By the mid-forties, he had moved to Norton, Ohio, where he became the marching band and choir director in the Wadsworth school system, as well as the organist for the Wadsworth Evangelical and Reformed Church. During his career, which lasted into the early seventies, he was obviously happy that his students could attend world-class events at a reasonable price. He regularly took students to Tuesday Musical concerts in nearby Akron. Yockey had one sibling, Eva Mae, who lived in Dover, Ohio. She probably attended several Tuesday Musical concerts (in fact, a 1968 *Akron Beacon Journal* article pictures both Arden and Eva together at an armory concert featuring the Cleveland Orchestra, see page 148). It appears that her brother stressed to her how important the events were for his students. In 1997, Eva Mae, somewhat of a recluse, passed away. Her last act, however, sent loud cheers through Akron's musical community.

Eva Mae turned out to be the 'Millionaire Next Door.' Through wise and steady investments, she had accumulated a substantial sum, and she had no immediate relatives to inherit the amount. She bequeathed over $500,000 to the club in memory of her brother, a sum ten times more than Tuesday Musical had ever received. The money was earmarked for the scholarship fund. The club was in an enviable position and was able to reward additional aspiring young musicians using the Arden J. Yockey scholarships for piano, strings, brass, woodwind, and voice.

In 1955, the club awarded only about $600 in scholarships. In 1957, the club had $2,000 to give to aspiring musicians—including the University of Akron Scholarship, which amounted to $50 per semester. By 1978, the club had provided over $50,000 to local college-aged students. Due to the Yockey bequest, the club awarded over $33,000 in scholarships in 2002 alone. In 2008, the club provided nearly $28,000 to deserving musicians. While scholarship endowments have been affected by the downturn in the US economy, Tuesday Musical has been able to maintain the level of awards at approximately $20,000 annually from 2010 through 2012.

Although Gertrude Seiberling did not live to see the outcome, along with scholarships, the post-World War II club extended a student-related activity that she would have endorsed—since it was modeled on a group she began in 1921. In February of that year, Seiberling, along with her daughter Irene Seiberling Harrison, invited fifteen young women to Gray Lodge to discuss setting up a Tuesday Musical auxiliary. (Gray Lodge was then the home of Goodyear President George Stadelman and today the Akron Woman's City Club occupies the building). The St. Cecelia Choral Society was initially for daughters and daughters-in-law of club members. A subsequent society constitution laid out member requirements: "Any young woman who is interested in music may, upon invitation of the Society and by passing the tests prescribed by the examining committee, become a member of the Society" ("Constitution of St. Cecelia Choral Society of Akron, Ohio," Tuesday Musical Collection, University of Akron Archives). The document also called for an active membership of not more than forty. St. Cecilia continues to perform several recitals annually.

In 1949, two more clubs for young musicians were organized as additional auxiliaries to Tuesday Musical. The Brahms Junior Music Club was for boys and girls in grades five through eight and the Allegro Youth Music Club was for boys and girls in grades nine through twelve. These clubs met monthly for programs and each club gave an annual spring recital. The clubs were an avenue to help young performers hone their skills and musical appreciation. While the Beatles might have preoccupied teenagers in the early sixties, the Brahms Junior Club members presented a program of "Patriotic Songs of America" after reading biographies of appropriate composers and the history of songs like "Yankee Doodle" and "America." The Allegro Club presented a recital at the Akron Art Institute (now the Akron Art Museum) in 1963 with the theme "Let the World Rejoice with Music." Eventually, by the late 1980s, the two clubs had merged into the Brahms Allegro Club, which was open to all area students from grades one through twelve who were studying music of any kind. The group scheduled regular meetings to share musical experiences, perform for each other, hear guest soloists and speakers, and take field trips to music-related facilities. As music entered into the digital age, the Brahms Allegro Club even invited musicians very familiar with computer-generated music to make presentations to the club members.

Women in Music History

1954: Peggy Glanville-Hicks's opera *The Transposed Heads* has its premier (in a concert version) at the Louisville Symphony.

1963: Esther Ballou's Capriccio for Violin and Piano is the first work by a female composer to premiere at the White House.

1968: Jazz pianist and composer Mary Lou Williams' *Music for Peace*, later known as *Mary Lou's Mass*, is commissioned by the Vatican.

Since the late 1940s, over thirty ladies have been elected president of Tuesday Musical's executive board. The orderly succession shows how effective the club has been at continuing its work. Many, if not all, of them played other roles in the club prior to becoming presidents of the board. Their experience aided them well in overseeing concerts and other club matters.

Wisely, in 1956 the club presented a young Van Cliburn to Akronites and got him at the ridiculously low cost of $750 (or $500, accounts vary) for his performance. When he returned in 1963, the well-known pianist cost the club around $6,000, and some club members thought his earlier performance was the better of the two.

Tuesday Musical's April 1957 Cleveland Orchestra concert was conducted by George Szell, featuring works by Berlioz, Debussy, and Tchaikovsky. After taking over the helm of the orchestra in 1946, Szell transformed the group from an excellent regional ensemble to one of the finest orchestras in the world. The Akron concert was a prelude to the orchestra's first European tour under the direction of Szell, an event that would vault the musicians to prominence that has grown through the decades.

The club celebrated its seventieth anniversary in 1957 and its eightieth anniversary in 1967. The club's 1968–69 season continued the tradition of bringing bold and imaginative artists to the area. The Spanish pianist Alicia De Larrocha, esteemed for her elegant Mozart performances and regarded as the greatest Spanish pianist in history, performed. The Korean violinist, Unk Kim gave a concert. Christoph Eschenbach, the German pianist making his American debut with the Cleveland Orchestra, took the stage for the club. Again, as had happened in the early years, some concerts were sold out and the club was forced to turn people away.

As the club neared the celebration of its ninetieth year, the Akron Armory had been the primary venue for Tuesday Musical evening concerts for over fifty years. The cavernous space saw many famous performers grace its stage, but by the 1960s the building was more than showing its age. Akron was in need of a better performance space. As one Tuesday Musical concert manager put it, at the armory "you could see people going to the bathroom and you could hear the toilet flushing" (Tuesday Musical Collection, University of Akron Archives). The ladies of the club had to do periodic spraying for insects to ensure dressing rooms were bug free when performers showed up for concerts, and because the facility was used by many different organizations, a previous night's performance, like the circus, left patrons with the aroma of peanuts and elephants. The city of Akron and The University of Akron also identified a need for a new home for the area's musical events and other artistic offerings and worked together to generate funding for a new building.

Tuesday Musical, because of money it had received in the late 1930s from Mary Schumacher, was able to assist with the funding necessary for the planned Center for the Performing Arts (later named the Edwin J. Thomas Performing Arts Hall). In May 1968, club president Alice Stempel handed over a check in the amount of $25,000 to the president of The University of Akron, Dr. Norman Auburn. The gift was placed in the Challenge '70 fund, the primary holding account for the building. At the same time, through donations of individual members, the club was able to augment the Schumacher Fund amount with an additional $1,300.

In 1973, the $13.9 million multi-use hall opened. To suit a variety of events, the hall was configurable as a 3,000-seat concert hall, a 2,400-seat theater, or a 900-seat recital hall. The stage could be adjusted as needed for the different seating arrangements. However, the most compelling aspect of the new hall was the sound system that blocked all outdoor noise and was able to capture sound intensity that varied by only three or four decibels anywhere in the house (*Cleveland Plain Dealer*, September 2, 1973). The state-of-the-art facility was an invitation to artists to come and perform and the club now had options to facilitate larger and smaller events.

The building of E. J. Thomas Hall was a victory for the city and the club, but the accomplishment was soon overshadowed by economic events in the late 1970s. In March 1978, Goodyear closed one of its bias-ply tire plants, leaving twelve hundred Akronites without jobs. In June, Firestone followed suit, furloughing almost the same number of workers. In August, thirteen hundred workers in another Firestone plant were asked to take pay cuts, but were not given assurances about their futures. In November, Mohawk Rubber closed its Akron plant. Another 318 workers faced uncertainty. Finally, rounding out the bad news, in a December announcement General Tire said it was closing its Akron plant.

The Akron closings were a precursor to the early 1980s recession, which saw Ohio lose almost five hundred thousand jobs or more than 10 percent of its total workforce—this accounted for about 20 percent of the entire country's job losses. Unemployment in Ohio peaked near 14 percent at the beginning of the decade and the annual rate of inflation in the early 1980s was over 10 percent.

Tuesday Musical had faced tough economic times previously, and luckily the club's finances had been augmented by the growth of the Schumacher endowment and gifts from the John S. and James L. Knight Foundation, among others. Still, costs were going to rise for the club's events. Artist fees and rent at E. J. Thomas were being driven by inflation. The stagehands union was asking for more money each year. The costs to print programs and advertise were skyrocketing. The club imposed a small price increase on season ticket prices, but also addressed the situation in a more concerted way.

In 1979, Dr. Bruce Rothmann, a pediatric surgeon and the husband of Lola Rothmann, the concert manager at the time, created a Concert Guarantors Fund to help subsidize the spiraling costs of concert programming. Bruce Rothmann was spurred to intervene because as he put it, "I constantly heard of the difficulties the club was experiencing in order to present the same quality of artists they had been presenting for nearly a century. So I suggested and volunteered ... I would begin a fund to help cover the cost of the concerts" (Tuesday Musical Collection, University of Akron Archives). With the goal of creating reliable capital for coming years, Rothmann invited some friends to his home to discuss his proposal. The group included Robert Crawford, the head of Crawford Printing Company and a concert enthusiast, and his wife Frances; Carolyn Frye Ryan, and her husband at the time, Roger; Margaret and Earl Baxtresser; Mabel and Dr. Lawrence Graham, a Silver Lake dentist. All viewed Tuesday Musical as a vital part of Akron's cultural heritage. Previously, Mabel Graham had provided the impetus, spurred on by a contribution of $500 from the *Akron Beacon Journal* manager John Barry, to raise enough money to create the Akron Symphony. Graham also served as president of Tuesday Musical Club from 1977–81 and received the club's Lola Rothmann Volunteer Achievement Award in 1981.

Within a short time, this group expanded to include Ralph and Sue Gillman and David and Margaret Hunter. Ralph was the Superintendent of the Summit County School System, David was an area attorney, and Sue and Margaret were both Tuesday Musical members. Each couple was asked to contribute $500 to seed the Fund, and they did so without question. In order to reach the goal of $1 million, the fund organizers "put a description of it in every concert program with a letter from me [Bruce Rothmann] telling what was going on and [asking] would you please support it. ... [I]t was amazing how many people responded to the ad in the program and sent us money. In addition to that, we had a couple of events: we kept promulgating this and I think for the first time we went to a number of foundations in town and to the GAR Foundation [named for Galen and Ruth Roush, founders of Roadway Express], as well" (Tuesday Musical Collection, University of Akron Archives). Funding reached the original goal amount and in fact doubled over time. Again as witnessed over the course of Tuesday Musical's history, when a financial need arose, Akron's patrons of the arts responded with a solution to keep the music playing.

Another event that aided Tuesday Musical's quest for greater financial stability came in the form of a grant from the John S. & James L. Knight Foundation. Tuesday Musical used the funding to establish the Clara I. Knight Young Artist Concert, named for Clara I. Knight, the mother of newspaper giants John S. and James L. Knight, and an enthusiastic supporter of the club. Young artists like Joshua Bell, Dina Kuznetsova, Jean Yves Thibaudet, Stephen Hough, Harlem Quartet, Hilary Hahn and Joshua Roman, among others, have performed. These musicians have gone on to have brilliant performing careers.

When an organization can overcome the ups and downs of business cycles, it should come as no surprise that individuals have given uncountable hours of time and effort for a specific cause. In the area of fund-raising, following in the early footsteps of Gertrude Seiberling and others was the late Jane Kaufman. An English composition teacher at The University of Akron from 1963 until her death in 2001, she was heavily involved in the Akron classical music scene, leading a successful effort to organize and fund the Akron Symphony Orchestra. She also was a key fund raiser for Tuesday Musical. Kaufman said of herself, "Everything I do, I do 150 percent, I don't dabble" (*Akron Beacon Journal*, October 22, 2001). In fact, she had taught her English composition class the morning of her death. Sherry Yoke, who served as Tuesday Musical's executive secretary from 1991 to 2000 was even more direct about Kaufman's persuasive skills. "There were a lot of talented women who worked their fannies off, but Jane would go to lunch and come back with $25,000. She might raise another $10,000 that afternoon. She knew a lot of people and she could persuade them to make big contributions to Tuesday Musical" (Tuesday Musical Collection, University of Akron Archives).

Even as resources continued to grow for Tuesday Musical, the club finances were reflective of "a penny saved is a penny earned" philosophy. New programs, new grant proposals, and additional awards increased the time volunteers needed to give. As more women entered the workforce or found themselves more involved with their children's extracurricular activities, volunteer hours became more limited. In

1965, the governing board of Tuesday Musical decided to find permanent office space and hire an office manager. After much discussion about the pros and cons of expending capital for the arrangements, a yearly amount of $600 was allocated for space at Stan Hywet and an additional $350 budgeted to hire an office manager. Looking to economize as always, members donated green stamps for the purchase of a coffee pot!

Securing a Sound Future

PERHAPS THE MOST SIGNIFICANT exercise the club undertook in the last several decades was the 1998 external review it sought. While the endowment funds were financially stable, decreased concert attendance had become an issue. By 1998, subscribers to the annual concert series had reached a low of 770, and of that number 462 were over the age of sixty. Major funders of Tuesday Musical events were beginning to question the value of their investments as fewer people came to concerts. The list of performers was still top notch, but the general public viewed the organization as "stuffy and behind the times" (Management Consultants for the Arts, Inc., "Summary Analysis: Tuesday Musical Club," December 7, 1998).

Betty Sloan, the president of Tuesday Musical at the time, and an ad hoc committee of members took the unprecedented step of hiring an outside firm to perform a thorough review of the organization. Previously, when the club had faced challenges, the membership provided solutions and strategies to implement necessary changes. In fact, many club members didn't see a need to alter that practice or recognize that the club was actually facing a crisis at all. However, the executive board gave the go-ahead and Gregory Kandel and the Connecticut-based Management Consultants for the Arts (MCA) were retained for the study. Perhaps the club chose MCA because of its philosophy—"We have found that the most successful organizations embrace their missions and are driven by them. This is not at the expense of bottom line objectives. When programmatic and artistic goals are the overriding concern; that is, when they are exciting, vital, and viable, all else follows, including financial return" (MCA website).

The move to hire an outside consultancy firm also reflected the new realities Akron and Tuesday Musical faced at the end of the twentieth century. The city itself had seen its population decline from around 275,000 residents in 1950 to fewer than 220,000 by 2000. The two-earner family was also impacting the time any volunteer could spend on club activities. And of course, the advent of technology that allowed for extreme personalization and instant gratification was a factor in the decline in concert attendance.

The review by MCA was not open-ended. The club had insisted that two priorities be kept in mind as the analysis took place—volunteerism needed to continue, but programs outside of the concert series did not have to be volunteer run, and the concert series had to continue under the independent aegis of the club. With these factors in mind, MCA spoke with about 120 people familiar with Tuesday Musical and tried to answer three critical questions.

1. Does the club need to hire a salaried executive director?
2. How many concerts should be part of the club's annual program?
3. Is it time to change how the club is governed?

Twelve recommendations came out of MCA's investigation. The extent that Tuesday Musical decided to accept these points has shaped the history of the organization to the present. Since volunteerism was a cornerstone in the founding and continuous operation of the organization, it needed to be reemphasized in the organization's mission statement. Even though a small office made up of paid staff had been created, Tuesday Musical's operations for present and future were still to be driven by volunteer services provided by its members.

The second recommendation dealt with protecting the reputation of Tuesday Musical's concert series. In the short term, even though the club's endowment fund would be drawn down, the club was advised to schedule artists more recognizable to the general public . The club was very good at identifying rising stars, but perhaps a greater emphasis on famous artists would revive interest in the series and increase ticket sales.

Coupled with the second recommendation was the following one, which advised the club to cut back its series from seven concerts per season to five or six. The ripple effect would lessen the workload on volunteers, while also providing additional funding for name artists. Potential subscribers might be more inclined to sign up for an entire season subscription if one or two artists interested them. Further, funders of specific events would be pleased because seats would be filled.

One of the more controversial ideas resulted from recommendations four and five—the club should limit the appearance of the Cleveland Orchestra in future years. The orchestra had been a mainstay of each Tuesday Musical season but one since the orchestra's founding. Unfortunately, the orchestra's appearance also saddled the club with its biggest net loss, which equated to 35 percent of the total operating loss of the full concert series.

The sixth recommendation called for an increase in scholarship levels, coupled with better publicity for the scholarship program in general. If more people were made aware of the club's outreach to young musicians, more donors might be willing to support these activities. The club was also urged to continue offering complimentary and discounted tickets to students in order to build subscribers for the future.

Understanding that active participation resulted in a better organization in general, MCA suggested limiting member's meetings to six or eight times a year. The commitment needed for monthly meetings was severely impacted by the amount of time members needed to attend to other activities. As the report noted, "[t]he bottom line is that it will be better to have less meetings, all well attended, than holding an arbitrary number and continuing to face difficulty in finding programs and venues" (Management Consultants for the Arts, Inc., "Summary Analysis").

Because one of the "most powerful tools in raising money and selling tickets" (Management Consultants for the Arts, Inc., "Summary Analysis") is an organization's image and position in the marketplace, the next recommendation revolved around marketing. Tuesday Musical had relied on volunteer-driven ticket sales, which was helpful in many ways, but limited the media footprint of the club. Competition had also increased—E. J. Thomas Hall was doing five times more programming than it had only seven years before. Cleveland's Playhouse Square had increased its offering and presence in the Akron market and the Akron Symphony had a following of its own. Tuesday Musical needed a fresh image, a more modern promotional and sales strategy, and a marketing operation that was not part of the concert manager's responsibilities.

Coupled with marketing was a need to professionalize the club's fund-raising. As indicated in recommendation nine, since increasing ticket sales was a multiyear process, a strategy to raise greater subsidies was something that could be planned immediately. MCA suggested forming a corporate leadership council of prominent local business executives and appointing a chair of development, rather than having the position go to the immediate past president, especially if that person was not completely committed to the activity.

At the time of the analysis, MCA recognized that Tuesday Musical's finances were relatively sound for an operation of its type. Still, the concert series was losing money, even with sponsorships. The club was aware that increasing subscriptions to 1,100 would not completely fund the concert series. Recommendation ten called for a more transparent and easily understood budget that linked all categories of financial support to specific line items. This would help Tuesday Musical members better understand the financial obligations of the organization and how revenue was keeping up with expenses. Also, MCA suggested that the club's financial advisors present alternative strategies to grow the club's endowment, instead of being required to design a specific return to cover the club's annual financial gap.

The last two recommendations involved the club's organizational structure. The first, recommendation eleven, dealt with the club's various committees. Since Tuesday Musical grew in an evolutionary manner, MCA suggested codifying the purpose of each committee. After this was done, committee work could be reviewed to see how well annual goals were met. Further, MCA saw a need to review the club's presidential term and recommended that it be changed from a two-year to a three-year term. This would allow the president to launch and implement initiatives. Several suggestions to help redistribute the workload of volunteers were also identified.

The final piece that MCA identified in its look at the club was to immediately outsource the marketing and public relations of the club and hire permanent staff. The latter action was supported by many of the club's major funders, but was a contentious issue among the club's membership. While not explicitly suggesting that the club needed a paid executive director, MCA did indicate that due to the many day-to-day activities, including working with an external marketing firm, volunteers could not likely accomplish these tasks with regularity.

In conclusion, Kandel understood that even though the many changes he suggested would seem aggressive to some club members, the time had come to implement a new path. As he noted:

> I am frankly inspired by the history of quality produced by essentially volunteer support. The organization's people and the community should be proud. ... I feel sure that the efforts of the past century by many generations to make Tuesday Musical as special as it is will be continued. Tuesday Musical *will* be successful if major changes in the concert series are embraced and if reinforcements through paid support and strengthened volunteer structures are put in place. (Management Consultants for the Arts, Inc., "Summary Analysis")

Tuesday Musical's response came in a variety of areas, and as of today, the framework of the organization and its programmatic offerings are still being adapted to changing situations. One of the club's first responses was to change its mission statement, as well as its name to Tuesday Musical Association, to emphasize the volunteer nature of the organization. As currently stated, "The Mission of Tuesday Musical Association, *as a volunteer-managed* [emphasis added] non-profit classical music organization, is to provide a premier concert series for the community, a comprehensive educational and scholarship program for young people, and performing and listening opportunities for its members and guests" (Tuesday Musical website, 2013).

Tuesday Musical also realized the need to take a risk and program more 'superstar' musicians in the concert series. This would increase the organization's visibility in the community, as well as increase both subscription and single ticket sales.

Luckily, Tuesday Musical could rely on its concert manager to do much of the scheduling of artists and negotiating of contracts. In fact, the concert manager, a volunteer position until the early 1970s, became the stable force during the modern era of the organization. If Gertrude Seiberling was the face of the club until the early 1940s, Lola Rothmann and Barbara Feld have provided the seasonal glue for the last four decades.

Lola Rothmann began her stint as concert manager in 1971. She scheduled and organized Tuesday Musical concerts until 1989. Even though Tuesday Musical had moved its office from Stan Hywet's carriage house to E. J. Thomas Hall in 1973, Rothmann spent more of her time elsewhere taking care of bookings and artists' needs. Rothmann, who had worked for the Akron Symphony Orchestra, was quite direct in how she learned about concert management. "Some people go to college to take administration courses. I didn't. I had on-the-job-training." She admits that on her first booking trip to New York City that she "was scared to death" (Tuesday Musical Collection, University of Akron Archives). The experience only strengthened her resolve and spirit to learn more.

Over her eighteen years of service, Rothmann dealt with emergencies and eccentricities. Almost immediately on taking the position, Rothmann was faced with a stranded performer. On January 21, 1971, Lili Chookasian, a principal singer with the Metropolitan Opera, was scheduled to perform in Akron. The roads from Youngstown to Akron were treacherous and the weather kept many concertgoers at home, reducing the crowd to about three hundred people. A call from Chookasian prior to the show let Rothmann know her arrival would be extremely close to curtain time. The Met star arrived, walked on stage with hamburger in hand, asked the audience to all move down front, told them she needed to eat and change, and would be out as soon as possible. The show went on and the concert was great, according to Rothmann.

Rothmann travelled to greater lengths to ensure that Joan Sutherland, one of the most acclaimed sopranos of the twentieth century, made her Akron date. A snowstorm in Rochester, New York, was about to force Sutherland to cancel her Akron event. Rothmann commandeered a local company's plane, flew to Rochester in inclement weather, and brought the soprano back to Akron for her performance.

A presentation of the BayaniHan Philippine Dancers presented a special challenge for Rothmann. Part of their routine included dancing with lit torches. The Akron Armory's manager saw this as a possible safety hazard, not to the audience but to the building itself. Rothmann arranged for firemen to be present, with filled buckets in hand, in case anything went wrong, and thankfully nothing did.

Concert managers, like Rothmann, also tread a fine line between pleasing members and scheduling great talent. Some club members resisted booking Israeli violinist Itzhak Perlman or classical pianist Andre Watts. Luciano Pavarotti, who set the standard for operatic tenors of the post-World War II era, might have riled some of the members because he had crossed over into the popular music realm, but for Rothmann, "he was very charming and complimentary to us and sang a nice recital to a packed house" (Tuesday Musical Collection, University of Akron Archives).

Women in Music History

1975: Musicologist Janet Knapp becomes the first female president of the American Musicological Society.

1997: The Vienna Philharmonic Orchestra votes to accept women members of the orchestra.

2000: Jessye Norman sings the premier of Judith Weir's *woman.life.song* at Carnegie Hall.

2011: Judith Weir's opera *Miss Fortune* is performed at the Bregenz Festival.

Barbara Feld succeeded Lola Rothmann as Tuesday Musical concert manager for the 1989–90 season. Feld remembers several unusual situations that needed to be addressed over the years. In 1997, Cecilia Bartoli, an Italian coloratura mezzo-soprano opera singer and recitalist, was scheduled to perform as part of a collaborative effort between Tuesday Musical and E. J. Thomas Hall. Bartoli and her non-English speaking string quartet arrived at Feld's doorstep in a mobile home. Not only were they hungry, but they were all coming down with the flu. Feld quickly got them to a doctor and then took them to a local market to get staples and a pot for soup making. It was a superb performance to a sold-out house.

In 2008, Lawrence Brownlee, an in-demand bel canto tenor from nearby Youngstown, had an extended stay in Akron. Brownlee and his pianist Martin Katz arrived the night before the concert and next day's weather forecast called for snow. By morning, all area schools and universities were closed. Tuesday Musical volunteers called all subscribers to let them know the concert had been rescheduled for the following night. Tuesday Musical did manage to hold Brownlee's master class, as well as one by Katz, and all students able to attend got extra coaching. Six hundred patrons managed to arrive the next evening to hear Brownlee sing and even though the weather was frightful, Brownlee was delightful.

Feld remembers feeding Itzhak Perlman at Swenson's, a local Akron drive-in which features the award-winning Galley Boy, a cheeseburger with two special sauces. She paid Russian baritone Dmitri Hvorostovsky during the intermission of his performance and had to do so in cash. The singer promptly put the wad of bills in his boots and went on with the show. Two performers requested prime seats for their dogs. Sometimes, as Feld notes, the best intentions aren't successful. The Kronos Quartet's atonal offering sent half the audience home at intermission.

Tuesday Musical was ever mindful that it must continue to present the 'best of the best.' The proposition had its financial risks, but in order to remain healthy as an organization and contribute to the cultural fabric of the community, more people had to become acquainted with all varieties of quality music. The process never stops.

The September 20, 2011 concert featuring world-class trumpeter Wynton Marsalis and the Jazz at Lincoln Center Orchestra was reflective of the organization's programmatic evolution. Almost three thousand area music lovers came out that night, many undoubtedly first-time concertgoers. In addition, nine hundred Northeast Ohio students attended the concert at no cost as part of Tuesday Musical's voucher program. As if the evening would never stop, at a postconcert reception in E. J. Thomas's BF Goodrich Lobby, Marsalis gave an impromptu performance with a local jazz ensemble who had entertained the guests before Marsalis arrived. The bass player with the local jazz group was a young student from The University of Akron who also participated in a master class the following day. Feld and Tuesday Musical were overjoyed. "It was one of the most brilliant musical experiences from beginning to end," Feld recalled (Tuesday Musical Collection, University of Akron Archives).

Beginning with the 2003–04 season, Tuesday Musical presented six, rather than seven, concerts. That season featured the pianist Lang Lang, as well as Yo-Yo Ma and the Silk Road Ensemble. Tuesday Musical has gone on to present Yo-Yo Ma in recital with Kathryn Stott and it brought back Yo-Yo Ma and the Silk Road Ensemble for the 125th anniversary season (2013). As part of a successful marketing initiative, the organization has offered new season subscribers a 50 percent reduction off the cost of a regular subscription and when subscribers renew for a second year, they receive a 25 percent reduction. Traditionally, all concerts were on a Tuesday night; however, due to the increasing demands of scheduling both the artists and E. J. Thomas Hall, it became necessary to be more flexible.

While Kandel had reservations about continuing the yearly performance of the Cleveland Orchestra, Tuesday Musical never wanted to discontinue presenting this world-class ensemble. Feld met with Jonathan Martin, then the general manager of the orchestra, to discuss this long-standing relationship. Martin wrote a letter to the organization assuring all members how important it was for the orchestra and musicians to be part of the series each year. The Cleveland Orchestra continues to perform annually, with student attendance increasing each year.

Tuesday Musical began to take active steps to enhance its image and broaden its impact in the local community in order to expand its audience base. Its student voucher program is under the education umbrella and is one of the organization's most successful education outreach strategies. The program has allowed more than twenty thousand regional students to attend concerts at no cost. Additionally, if schools or groups bring more than twenty students, the cost of transportation is covered by the organization.

Education outreach also includes visits by the artists to area schools for master classes, residencies, and lecture/demonstrations. This award-winning initiative enhances and promotes music education to a greater demographic of the community. A prime example followed the October 2, 2007 concert by the Grammy-winning vocal ensemble Chanticleer. In cooperation with the John S. and James L. Knight Foundation, more than three hundred students from local high schools spent an entire day with members of Chanticleer, who coached them in vocal technique, stage etiquette, and ensemble singing. As a final part of the day-long residency, the high school choirs performed individually and en masse with Chanticleer at St. Bernard's Catholic Church in downtown Akron. The concert was free and open to the public, with a full house once the concert began.

During the 2005–06 season, Imani Winds, one of the most successful woodwind chamber music ensembles in the world, visited local schools and performed for students. The African American ensemble worked with a local not-for-profit group, Project GRAD Akron. The latter organization's mission, in part, is to "ensure a quality public school education for all at-risk children in economically disadvantaged communities" (Project GRAD Akron website).

The extraordinary cellist Joshua Roman, who did his formal training at the Cleveland Institute of Music, was a part of Tuesday Musical's outreach program during the 2011–12 season. In addition to his master class with university students and his lecture/demonstration with middle school students, he also took his outreach into the community. Roman played for patients at the Summa Health System Infusion Lobby. Several of the relatives spoke with Roman and told him what his playing had meant to their relatives and expressed deep gratitude for his mini-performance. It goes without saying that many who heard him could not attend his concert due to illness. However, this mini-concert was something that deeply touched those present.

The educational outreach program represents one initiative to help aspiring musicians. The other, of course, is Tuesday Musical's scholarship program. As mentioned previously, the Yockey bequest has been a large factor in increasing funds allocated to scholarships. Tuesday Musical members have also provided varying amounts to augment this beneficial endeavor.

Although not all programs succeed, the advantages of trying are just as important. During the 1990 season, Tuesday Musical and The University of Akron School of Music joined together to collaborate on "a fully produced opera using the talented voices in the department and a professional star system for one or two lead roles" (Tuesday Musical Collection, University of Akron Archives). The first production was *La Traviata* with Alfred Anderson, the university's director of opera and musical theatre, singing the baritone role of the elder Germont. The production also introduced the Tuesday Musical audience to soprano Dina Kuznetsova, a graduate student at The University of Akron, who has gone on to an international operatic career.

The collaboration resulted in the productions of *Rigoletto* (1992), *Tosca* (1994), *Carmen* (1996), and *The Magic Flute* (1998). Rising costs eventually ended the series, but the benefits were undeniable. Young musicians were able to meet, learn from, and perform with professional singers. Audiences were afforded the chance to see full-scale opera presentations, musical events that were not readily available to Akron audiences.

Beginning in 2009, another collaboration resulted in the *FUZE!* Series, which featured musicians who were classically trained, but pushed the boundaries of classical music and, in the process, tested new musical frontiers. In collaboration with the Akron Art Museum, performances were held in the museum's intimate 160-seat Lehner auditorium. The inaugural concert brought the innovative string quartet ETHEL to the area for a performance with an eye on tradition and an ear to the future. Other performers included Brooklyn Rider (described by Fred Child at NPR as "young musicians … recreating the 300-year-old form of string quartet"); the Sixth Floor Trio ("Chamber music societies who would like to crack the windows and let a little air into stuffy concert series should give a listen to the Sixth Floor Trio," ClevelandClassical.com); and Daniel Bernard Roumain (the Haitian America composer known for fuzing classical music roots with a myriad of soundscapes). *FUZE!* attracted an enthusiastic younger generation of music lovers, along with regular concertgoers who loved new music.

The Kandel report recommended making some organizational changes while retaining an emphasis on volunteer work that started at 610 East Market Street in 1887. Tuesday Musical reduced its monthly meetings to a schedule of nine meetings each year, of which one is the scholarship recital held each May. The recital itself provides a larger impact for the scholarship program and provides a regular way to enhance media coverage for the association. For several years, the June meeting has been held at one of Akron's parks—hearkening back to earlier day when members gathered for summer picnics.

Since Tuesday Musical's administrative structure now includes paid staff, the members' meetings have been restructured. Typically, business issues are still discussed, but in a less time-consuming fashion. The remainder of the time is filled with music. Most gatherings feature performances by Tuesday Musical members or other area professional musicians. Frequently, scholarship winners or a Brahms Allegro member add to the entertainment. Members are always encouraged to bring guests and attendance at the meetings range from seventy-five to a hundred individuals.

In 1995, in a move that seemed to be irony turned on its head, while men's organizations were just allowing women to become members,

Tuesday Musical decided to recruit men for membership. David Fisher became the first Tuesday Musical male member. A pianist himself, David was the music director of the Ohio Ballet from 1974 to 2005. By 2006, the organization had elected its first male president, Jerry Davidson. He had been a faculty member of the Kent State University music department for twenty-seven years. Before assuming the presidency, he had been program chairman for the members' meetings and was editor of the newsletter.

Tuesday Musical also came to the realization that in order to provide stability and engender long-term planning, paid staffing was a necessity. After the analysis by MCA, Concert Manager Barbara Feld became the executive director and additional part-time support staff was added. Eventually, a full-time director of development was hired, in addition to the part-time business manager. The executive director reports to the executive board and staff reports to the executive director. The volunteer side of the organization, which includes the many operational committees, reports to the board through the president.

The way Tuesday Musical handles its executive positions and governance has made presidential transition easier. The president typically serves a two-year term, after serving two years as vice president. After the president's term is up, the individual remains on the board for another two years. Another step to better governance involved working with a local center for non-profit excellence. Beginning in 2013, a consultant worked with Tuesday Musical members and subscribers to develop a new three-year strategic plan.

Along with organizational improvements, Tuesday Musical is committed to a three-year budgeting process, as opposed to its traditional one-year plan. The organization has also revised its endowment spending policy, allowing for greater financial flexibility with its endowment fund.

Understanding that perception was reality, the most auspicious problem was to educate area residents about membership versus being a subscriber. Many thought being a musician was required for membership and at one time that was true. However, it became quite apparent in the late 1960s and early 1970s that membership had to be inclusive, rather than exclusive. The requirements for membership are few (no auditions and no classical music tests—just a love of great performances), but the rewards are great. Members must purchase an annual season subscription, plus pay a nominal annual fee. Membership benefits include attending the members' programs and the ability to bring guests. This practice reflects what the early founders envisioned for Tuesday Musical—an organization open to all who have a love for or would like to learn more about classical music. Today, Tuesday Musical Club is Tuesday Musical Association. For more than ten years, Tuesday Musical has worked with the marketing firm Triad Communications to build a greater awareness of the organization and to help position it as one of the community's leading arts organizations. Doing so has allowed the group to provide a picture for its activities that was focused by a unified message. Having a visible and consistent look and feel for its programs reiterated the value of Tuesday Musical in the cultural life of Akron.

Of course, the messaging also helped with development activities. When an organization is able to have all members talk the same language, foundations, corporate sponsors, and individuals see a viable avenue for exposure. The new image also has resulted in an increase in the number of season subscribers. It is of interest and worth noting that tickets for the 1902 performance of Mme. Schumann-Heink cost two dollars, which adjusted for inflation, would have amounted to over to over fifty dollars today. Luckily, except for special concerts, individual tickets only cost between $25–$45.

The Next Century

THE LINEAGE OF CLASSICAL music in Akron began at 610 East Market Street, the location where Tuesday Musical started. Today that area is a hospital complex, the outgrowth of the Bartges house (converted into City Hospital in 1892) and a pharmacy stand near the home where Celia Baker held the planning meeting for the club. Another landmark of the era, the old Byron W. Robinson mansion built by the clay products mogul in 1906, now called Steinway Hall, houses a piano seller. The mansion, one of the last stately buildings that survived urban renewal, tells a larger story than the several fast-food locations that dot the neighboring properties. Gertrude Seiberling lived just up the road in 1887, at 512 East Market. The First Methodist Episcopal Church, where many of the early club programs were held, was destroyed by fire in 1911. The aptly named Church Street on which it was located no longer connects to Broadway and the site is occupied by Summit County court buildings.

The Goodyear Company was started twelve years after Tuesday Musical and though its manufacturing plants are no longer producing tires in Akron, its global headquarters are still located in town and stand about two miles from 512 East Market. Stan Hywet is no longer a residence, but visitors still pass through its gates to glimpse the property where Gertrude Seiberling strolled, tended garden, and might even have played golf on the course within the estate's walls. Ferdinand Schumacher's oats factory, purchased by The University of Akron, is now a dormitory for students and has office space as well. Lasell Academy later became Lasell College and opened its doors to men in 1997. Companies like Akron Varnish Company and the Akron Cracker Company are long gone.

The Beacon Publishing Company published the *Summit Beacon* in 1887, which eventually became the *Akron Beacon Journal.* In the early 1900s, Charles Landon Knight became publisher and owner of the *Akron Beacon Journal*, and along with his wife, the former Clara Scheifley, moved across town from the Seiberlings into a house at 502 West Market Street. John, a son of the Knights, became one of the paper's sportswriters in 1920, its managing editor in 1925, and its owner in 1933, when Charles died. John Knight expanded his newspaper empire, owning fifteen dailies by 1973. Eventually, he would become editorial chairman of the Knight-Ridder chain.

Along with his brother, James, John started the Knight Memorial Education Fund in 1940, to aid college students in the Akron area. The fund grew into the John S. and James L. Knight Foundation which "supports transformational ideas that promote quality journalism, advance media innovation, engage communities and foster the arts" (Knight Foundation website). The philanthropic vision of the Knight children was a gift of their mother, Clara, who was a supporter of Akron community and culture. Tuesday Musical, an organization that she admired, continues to celebrate her life as one example of the many women who contributed to the success of the club.

Akron's musical score has continued, with few rests, for over twelve decades. Like Akron itself, Tuesday Musical has made adjustments for the times and technologies. Each new season presents a challenge for the club's members and each concert is the result of many hands working in unison. Gertrude Seiberling might not have known how resourceful Tuesday Musical would become, but she surely understood what it would take to bring classical music to her city, "It is only when great numbers of people unite in one glorious ideal that a great movement can be successful" (*Papers and Proceedings of the Music Teachers' National Association*, 41st Annual Meeting, Philadelphia, December 29–31, 1919, pp. 108–12). The history of Tuesday Musical has been a chronicle of volunteers. Some worked on committees, some worked for a season or two, and some made Tuesday Musical a vital cog in their lives. They all worked for the music. Many more will continue the tradition, because as Henry David Thoreau noted, "music is perpetual, and only hearing is intermittent" (*The Writings of Henry David Thoreau*, Journal IX, edited by Bradford Torrey, Boston: Houghton Mifflin, 1906).

A Pictorial History

Sharon Cebula &
Cynthia L. Harrison

The Beginning, 1887–1903

ONE AFTERNOON in the fall of 1887, Celia Baker invited around a dozen friends to her home to discuss their shared love of music. These women were the wives and daughters of local business magnates, all well-educated, well-off, and eager to express their love of classical music. At this meeting, they formed the Tuesday Afternoon Club. Though loosely organized, Tuesday Afternoon Club was no mere social club; its members were trained musicians who braved rigorous auditions for the privilege of performing in club recitals. The members studied the masters of classical music and held small choral concerts in area churches for themselves and their families. Gertrude Ferguson Penfield Seiberling, who came to Akron as F. A.

Tuesday Afternoon Club, January 1888. First row, from left: Belle Brooker Luxmore, Jessica Wolfe Otis, Lillie May Burnham Saunders, Sybil Caskey Fair, Emma Motz Gehring. Second row, from left: Ione Edgerton, Martha Herrold Fitzpatrick, Celia Ashmun Baker, Gertrude Penfield Seiberling, Helen Storer Collins, Harriet Seiberling Miles. Third row, from left: Belle Bennett, Dorothy Bell, Zelle Adams Oviatt, May Bennett Wagner, Sarah Motz McCrum, Alma Little App, Frances Robinson Adams.

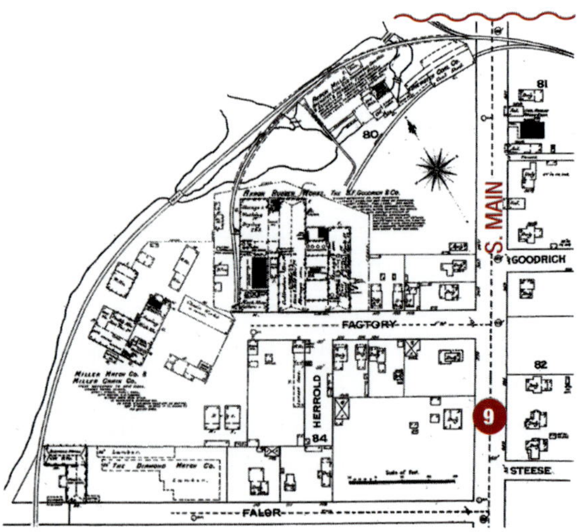

Where the Founders Lived

1. Celia Ashmun Baker
   610 E. Market*
2. Frances Robinson Adams
   300 Kent
3. Zelle Adams Oviatt
   306 Kent
4. Harriet Seiberling Miles
   202 Fir
5. Lillie May Burnham Saunders
   210 Fir
6. Alma Little App
   141 N. Broadway
7. Sarah Motz McCrum
   108 S. Broadway
8. Sybil Caskey Fair
   126 S. Broadway
9. Martha Herrold Fitzpatrick
   958 S. Main
10. Jessica Wolfe Otis
    Arcade Block, S. Howard
11. Lucy Ione Edgerton
    116 S. Walnut

*Site of first meeting

Downtown Akron, Ohio, circa 1887.
Map compiled by Lauren McAndrews

Seiberling's bride the month after the club first met, quickly became an enthusiastic member.

In 1890, Celia Baker moved to Colorado and by 1892 Helen Storer took over the direction of the club. Helen's first change was to invite the public to both the group's choral concerts and performances by visiting musicians. By 1894, a popular vote among members allowed men to join the chorus, and the mixed chorus enjoyed an era of great popularity. With membership in the hundreds and evening concerts that reliably filled the largest venues in the city, the club experienced exponential growth. Shortly after the turn of the century, the club incorporated and changed its name to Tuesday Musical Club. It was one of the city's preeminent providers of first-class musical entertainment from around the world.

In 1901, Helen Storer stepped down as director to marry Winfred Collins, though she continued to contribute to the town's musical life. A progression of directors followed, though none matched Helen's zeal and dedication. (In the club's early years, the head of the executive board carried the title of director; now this position carries the title of president.) When Charles Clemens of Cleveland took over, he moved the responsibility of ticket sales from the members, who were enthusiastic and familiar with their patrons, to an outside professional salesman. This practice and a period of lax support ultimately threatened the club's very existence. In the first years of the new century, members left and ticket sales declined. A slow recovery from a nationwide recession compounded the club's financial difficulties, and the club declared bankruptcy in 1902, cancelling all of its scheduled concerts. Not content to let the club fade away, a committee of members sent Gertrude Seiberling to the convention of the National Federation of

PROGRAM

Selection .... Foster's orchestra
"America," ....The Tuesday Musical club and the audience
Address by the chairman............ Mayor W. E. Young
"Greetings,"..First section read by Miss Antoinette Beard
"The Star Spangled Banner," ....
......Prof. N. L. Glover and The Tuesday Musical Club
Address .... Dr. W. C. Jacobs
Address .... Dr. W. W. Leonard
"Angel of Peace,"............. The Tuesday Musical Club
Address .... Hon. George W. Crouse
Tableau, "Battle Scene."
"Greetings," Second Stion read by Miss Maude Herndon
Tableau, "After the Battle."
Vocal Solo .... Mrs. F. A. Seiberling
Address .... Gen. Charles Dick
Tableau, "The Innocent Victim."
Address ....Ira A. Priest, D.D., President of Buchtel College
"The Flag Without a Stain .... White
Prof. N. L. Glover, S. D. Richards, W. C. Findley and C. W. Clark.
Greettings. Third Section read by Miss Carita McEbright.
Address .... Hon. N. D. Tibbals
Selection .... Liedertafel Society
Address .... Rev. T. F. Mahar
New Year's Hymn, "O, God Our Help in Ages Past"....
.... The Tuesday Musical Club
Address .... Rev. J. L. Davies
"Praise God, From Whom All Blessings Flow."
Benediction .... Rev. Charles Edward Keller
The Tuesday Musical Club is assisted by members of the church choirs of the city.

Red Cross Watch Night performance, December 31, 1900. From the *Akron Daily Democrat*, January 2, 1901

ANNUAL BANQUET

Of Tuesday Musical Club at Silver Lake.

A very pleasant outing Wednesday evening was that of the Tuesday Musical club at Silver Lake park. Members of the club and their friends, to the number of 200, attended and the evening passed away merrily with banqueting, singing and boating.

The banquet was prepared by the women of the club, who went to the park at 3:30 in the afternoon, and arranged the spread on the tables in one of the large dining halls. The men arrived at the park about 7 o'clock, when the banquet was served.

The steam boat was chartered and an hour or so was spent on the lake. Plantation songs and choruses were sung and the music was given an additional sweetness as it floated out over the water.

The only thing occurring to mar the pleasure of the event was when Miss Angie Watters fainted. Some time was required in restoring her to consciousness. Miss Watters has been in delicate health for some tim, but she is not much the worse of the outing today.

Music Clubs to look for ways to resuscitate the organization. What had seemed such a promising future was now uncertain at best. Implementing what she learned from the convention, Gertrude arrived at a possible solution: the club would form a People's Chorus. This magnificent ensemble, which would sing with the club's existing chorus, would consist of community members who could afford to pay the $2.00 membership dues. The club hoped this new inclusive approach would keep the community invested in Tuesday Musical's survival and buoy it through rough financial times.

Above, clockwise from top: Tuesday Musical members at the dedication of the First Methodist Church pipe organ, September 1896; From the *Akron Daily Democrat*, June 22, 1899

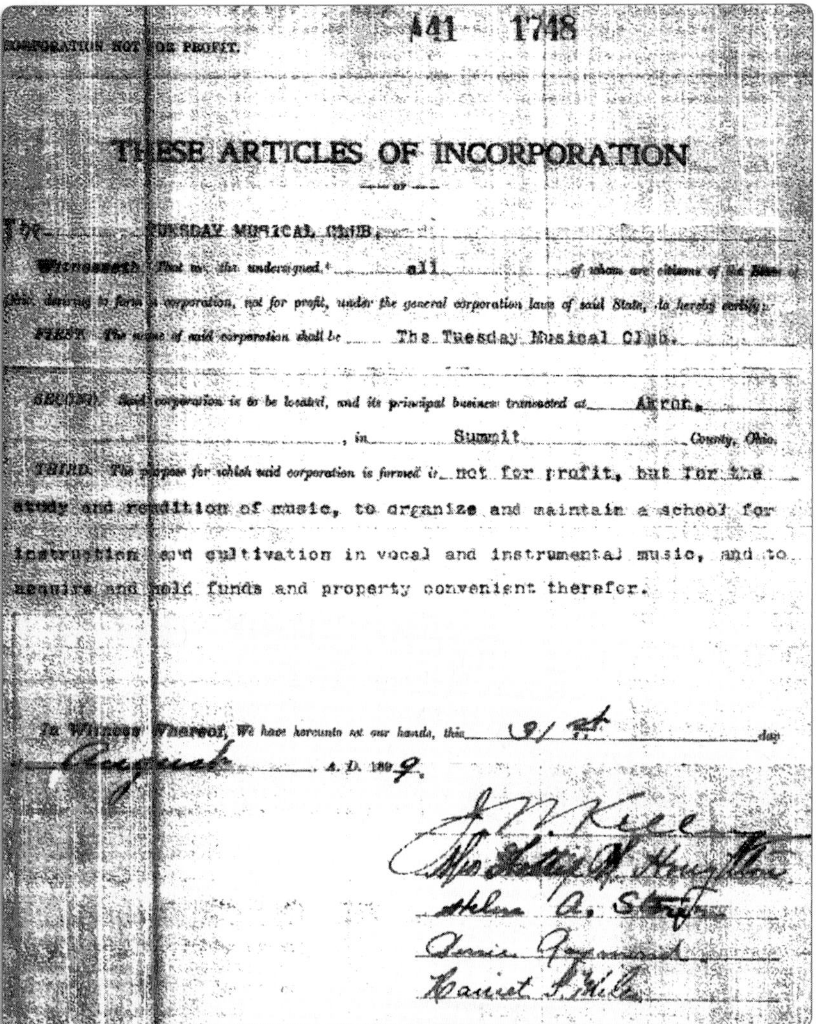

CORPORATION NOT FOR PROFIT.

441 1748

THESE ARTICLES OF INCORPORATION

— OF —

THE TUESDAY MUSICAL CLUB,

Witnesseth, That we, the undersigned, all of whom are citizens of the State of Ohio, desiring to form a corporation, not for profit, under the general corporation laws of said State, do hereby certify:

FIRST. The name of said corporation shall be The Tuesday Musical Club.

SECOND. Said corporation is to be located, and its principal business transacted at Akron, in Summit County, Ohio.

THIRD. The purpose for which said corporation is formed is not for profit, but for the study and rendition of music, to organize and maintain a school for instruction and cultivation in vocal and instrumental music, and to acquire and hold funds and property convenient therefor.

In Witness Whereof, We have hereunto set our hands, this 31st day August A.D. 1899.

J. W. Kelly
Miss Lottie M. Houghton
Helen A. Storer
Bessie Raymond
Harriet S. Miles

TUESDAY CLUB.

The Organization Has Been Formally Incorporated.

Incorporation papers were issued Wednesday to the Tuesday Musical club. The incorporators are: Mr. J. W. Kelly, Miss Lottie M. Houghton, Miss Bessie Raymond, Mrs. Harriet S. lMles and Mrs. Winfred B. Collins.

Above, clockwise from top: Articles of Incorporation from the Ohio Secretary of State, August 31, 1899; From the *Akron Daily Democrat*, January 30, 1901

Opposite, clockwise from top: From the *Akron Daily Democrat*, April 19, 1902; From the (Lincoln, NE) *Courier*, May 26, 1900; From the *Akron Daily Democrat*, September 23, 1899

Mme. Schumann-Heink!

The world renowned Contralto from the **Metropolitan Opera House,** New York City, in

Tuesday Musical Club Course,

MONDAY EVENING,

April 14th, at

First M. E. Church.

ADMISSION $2.00 Except to Course Ticket Holders.

The greatest Artist who has appeared in Akron.

Grand Organ Recital and Concert

Wednesday, Oct. 4, 1899

REOPENING OF THE GREAT ORGAN IN

First M.E. Church

OF AKRON

PROGRAMME

PART 1

1. "Be Not Afraid" (Elijah) .... Mendelssohn
   TUESDAY MUSICAL CLUB.
2. Organ, "Fantasie Originale" .... Wely
   MR. ARCHER.
3. Songs (a) "Where E'er You Walk" .... Handel
   (b) Morning Hymn (with organ accompaniment .... Henschel
   MRS. TALBOT.
4. Organ (a) Poeme Symphonique (Rouet d'Omphale) St. Saens
   (b) Concert Fugue in D .... Frederic Archer
   MR. ARCHER.
5. Trio (Violin, Piano and organ) Meditation (Faust) .... Guonod
   MR. VON KUNITS, HARRIET PARSONS
   MISS HENNEBERGER.

PART 2

1. Songs — Group of Love Songs.
   (a) "Thy Beaming Eyes" .... MacDowell
   (b) "Love's Philosophy" .... Cooke
   (c) "Since We Parted" .... Allitsen
   (d) "Ich Liebe Dich (I Love Thee" .... Grieg
   MRS. TALBOT.
2. Violin Solo .... To be selected
   MR. KUNITS.
3. Organ, Overture "Tannhauser" .... Wagner
   MR. ARCHER.
4. "He Watching Over Israel" (Elijah) .... Mendelssohn
   TUESDAY MUSICAL CLUB.
5. Invocation (with violin obligato) .... D'Hardelot
   MRS. TALBOT, MR. VON KUNITS
   Accompanied by piano and organ.

News of Woman's Clubs

A national federation of women's musical clubs appears to be an assured fact of the near future, says Harper's Bazar. The idea has been discussed since the World's Fair, during the continuance of which, as is well known, a very highly successful congress of such clubs was held. The occasional attempts, however, since 1893, to crystallize these clubs into a national body have not been successful in themselves, though they have stood for good pioneer work. At the meeting last June, in New York, of the National Association of Music Teachers, the woman's department of the convention most efficiently developed by Mrs. Sutro as president, seemed to offer the needed opportunity for the furtherance of the federation plan. One of the seven divisions into which Mrs. Sutro divided her department was that of Women's Musical Clubs, with Mrs. Charles S. Virgil of New York as chairman. Mrs. Virgil, in conducting her work, appointed a chairman from each state to report on the women's musical clubs from her state as part of the exhibit of this work at the New York congress. The marked interest which was taken in the matter and the response within a fortnight from over 200 clubs, rekindled the enthusiasm for the national body. This was further accentuated by an admirable paper read by Mrs. Chandler Starr of Rockford, Ill., on "A Review of the Congress of Women's Musi al Clubs at the World's Fair." Before the reading of Mrs. Starr's paper it was realized by some of the prominent club women in attendance at the convention that this paper would reopen the situation in a most suggestive way, and it was decided to make the effort at once, at the close of the day's program, to ascertain the feelings of the women present in regard to a national federation. In pursuance of this design a call for a meeting to discuss the matter was issued. Some of the women specially interested, besides Mrs. Sutro, Mrs. Virgil and Mrs. Starr, were Mrs. Russell H. Dow, president of the Schubert club of St. Paul, Minn.; Miss Marion F. Ralston of the Tuesday Musical club of St. Louis, Mo., and Miss Amy Fay, and many others. Mr. H. E. Krehbiel, the musical critic and writer, was also present, and in a pleasant little speech warmly advocated the matter, which he considered of great importance. In the enthusiasm of the afternoon it was voted to organize a temporary federation, which would be a working basis from which might spring later the permanent body. This was done, and Mrs. Sutro was made president, Mrs. Chandler Starr first vice president, Mrs. Russell H. Dow second vice president, Miss Marion F. Ralston secretary and treasurer. An executive board, assistant treasurer, auditor and one or two other minor officers were also appointed. This temporary body has, of course, no corporate status. The clubs which would naturally form the federation were by no means all represented, it was impossible to draft a constitution, and altogether, as has been said, the work was merely preliminary. Circulars, however, setting forth what has been done, and calling for an expression of opinion upon the matter as to the advisability of further effort, have been sent out by the secretary to every club that it was possible to reach throughout the country. The responses received indicate a strong and widespread interest. There will be a second meeting about the 1st of December, at some point not yet decided.

CELIA (CECELIA) ASHMUN BAKER was the hostess for the club's organizational meeting. The youngest daughter of Civil War surgeon Dr. George Parish Ashmun and former Lydia Wright was born April 29, 1851 in Hudson, Ohio. The family relocated in the 1870s to Akron, where she met Dr. George Griswold Baker of Norwalk, Ohio, who had joined her father's medical practice. Four months after their marriage on June 18, 1873, her father succumbed to illness related to war injuries suffered in a Confederate prison camp.

Dr. Baker sustained his growing family not only with his medical practice, but also as president of Akron Electric Light and Power, a precursor of Ohio Edison. In 1888, Celia left her membership with the club and their home on 610 East Market to establish a new life in Denver with her husband and their four surviving children. She enjoyed a scant eight years in Denver, dying March 8, 1896.

LUCY IONE EDGERTON (Ione) was another well-recognized member of the music community and founding member of the club. At the time of her birth in September 1867, her family had just returned to Akron from the western territories of Idaho and Montana, where her father, attorney Sidney Edgerton, had served as U.S. judge and then governor of the respective territories. Her mother, the former Mary Wright of Tallmadge, captured that historical period in a series of letters later assembled into *A Governor's Wife on the Mining Frontier: The Letters of Mary Edgerton from Montana.*

Ione was one of the noted couple's four daughters. She graduated from Oberlin Conservatory of Music with a Bachelor of Science degree; her elder sister Pauline became a chief administrator of the Akron Public Library. At the time of the club's founding she served as organist for Akron's First Congregational Church. Her musical talents were also utilized by Buchtel College; in 1903 she became an instructor of music. Her death on May 10, 1906 at her 235 Ely Street home after a brief illness was unexpected.

SARAH E. MOTZ MCCRUM (or Sadie) was a member of the 1883 Akron High School class, along with fellow founders Harriet (Hattie) Seiberling Miles and Helen Storer Collins. The daughter of life and fire insurance agent and American Cracker Company Vice President Henry Motz, Sarah started her married life on January 14, 1891, with the former insurance clerk John Homer McCrum. After his 1882 arrival in Akron, McCrum moved up in the ranks, from clerk to secretary and then treasurer of several varnish companies. By 1897, after a series of company mergers, he was treasurer of the Akron Varnish Company.

The McCrum home at 208 Adolph Avenue made Sarah a neighbor of several other club women, such as longtime member Elizabeth E. Eyster. Early in the summer of 1901, it became apparent that McCrum had mismanaged his employer's finances. With creditors filing suit for payment on everything from clothing to groceries, the family fled to England, Australia, and finally South America. Several months later, Sarah contacted legal representatives in an attempt to resolve matters on behalf of her ailing husband, citing a desire to return to the United States with her children. Although Sarah and her children visited her sister Emma Gehring in Cleveland, Ohio, numerous times after 1910, Sarah died June 18, 1933 in Buenos Aires, Argentina.

HELEN STORER COLLINS was, aside from Gertrude Seiberling, one of the most prominent members in shaping the early years of the club. She was also a classmate of Hattie Seiberling Miles and Sarah Motz McCrum. The daughter of Civil War veteran, city postmaster, and jeweler J. B. Storer, Helen was born May 23, 1867. In 1890, she received a Bachelor of Science in music from the Wellesley School of Music, Boston, and returned to the family home at 115 North High Street, where she became immersed in the active music scene of Akron. Not only was Helen the organist at St. Paul's Episcopal Church in Akron from 1893–95, but she subsequently directed its boys' choir from 1896–97.

Helen assumed the leadership of the club in 1892 and began membership expansion. Not content with involvement just around Akron,

Helen also attended the 1893 World's Fair Congress of Music Clubs in Chicago and the 1898 organizational meeting which chartered the National Federation of Music Clubs. At this latter meeting she was named as one of two directors for the Northern Middle Section of the National Federation of Music Clubs. Moving beyond regional representation in that organization, she became its recording secretary in 1901.

Helen married Winfred Collins on January 2, 1901. Collins, the son of a pharmacist, passed his druggist's licensing exam in 1899, but preferred to work in commerce. When he married Helen, he was the secretary-treasurer of the Akron Roofing and Tile Company. They resided near her parents at 17 North High and later established a residence called the Campania.

By 1903, Helen became the third president of the National Federation of Music Clubs. Under her direction, club expansion and the dissemination of education materials increased. Helen encouraged the admission of men and men's musical organizations, as well as establishing an artist bureau.

Much is unknown about her musical involvement following her illness in 1905. She died on December 14, 1917, in Cuyahoga County.

Tuesday Club Begin Work.

The first rehearsal of the Tuesday Musical club for this season was held Monday evening in the First Baptist church. Much spirit and enthusiasm were shown at the meetng. Mr. Clemens will again direct the club. The first number in the evening concert course will be the Pittsburg orchestra on Nov. 17. The Tuesday Musical club will sing two choruses at this concert.

Left: From the *Akron Daily Democrat*, September 16, 1902

Opposite, clockwise from top: From the *Akron Daily Democrat*, November 21, 1901; From the *Akron Daily Democrat*, October 29, 1902

REAL TREAT.

Tuesday Club's First Evening Concert.

Pittsburg Orchestra Pleased a Large Audience.

Under the auspices of the Tuesday Musical Club a real musical treat was afforded Akron music lovers by The Pittsburg Orchestra, Tuesday evening at the First M. E. church. Its rendition of the Masters, Beethoven and Wagner, has been unsurpassed in Akron, and Victor Herbert is indeed a fine leader. What was emphasized more than anything else was the perfect control he had over his men, by reason of which he was able to produce the very softest of tones with almost every man playing, or the longest music of Wagner. The audience was given a delightful taste of both in Beethoven's beautiful Symphony No. 4 in B flat, with its low, sweet singing tones, and the loud vibrant chords of Siegfield's Rhine Journey from Die Gollerdammerung of Wagner.

After the latter the audience was so insistent that Mr. Hubert gave another piece of Wagner's "Die Fraume." The parts "Puss in Boots and the White Cat," from Tscharkowsby's "Sleeping Beauty," and "Fete Nuptiale" by Hubert himself, seemed especially to please the large audience.

The mixed chorus of the club sang two numbers, "Lorelei" by Mendelssohn, with Mrs. Seabury C. Ford as soloist, and Faning's "Song of the Vikings."

The club certainly did itself proud and many expressions were heard that the members never before sang so well, nor were they so much enjoyed and Mr. Clemens received many congratulations for his excellent work.

Mrs. Ford has a very clear bird-like high soprano voice and she very much helped to make the concert one which would be well worth going a long way to hear.

MUSICAL

Season Opened by Tuesday Club.

A recital of modern violin music by Miss Caroline Harter, of Canton, assisted by Mr. Carey E. McAfee, pianist, of Wooster, for the study section of the Tuesday Musical club, marked the formal opening of the season of that organization in the Sunday school rooms of the First Baptist church Tuesday afternoon. The recital was in all respects excellent. Miss Harter possesses unusual talent which has been cultivated to a degree making her a thoroughly accomplished violinist. Mr. McAfee played with her perfectly. For several years he has been in the front rank, both as a pianist and organist, and both he and Miss Harter will be welcomed in Akron at any time.

Tuesday evening Miss Harter, Mr. McAfee, Mrs. F. A. Seiberling and Mrs. Chas. McDonald, of Cleveland, took part in an enjoyable musicale at the home of Mr. and Mrs. Geo. A. Barnes, Adolph ave.

The first evening concert of the Tuesday club will be given Nov. 17, when the Pittsburg orchestra, assisted by the mixed chorus of the club, will appear. The second concert will be a song recital by Mr. Herbert Witherspoon. A concert by the Philharmonic String Quartet of Cleveland, assisted by Mr. Chas. Bassett, pianist, and Mr. Narovec, clarionettist, will be the third event. The fourth concert will be given by well known soloists and the mixed chorus, and the fifth will be the usual May concert.

WHAT HAPPENED TO THE FOUNDING WOMEN?

Frances E. Robinson Adams

- Born in 1863, probably Akron, Ohio
- Died 1924, Akron, Ohio
- Married Frank Hyde Adams in 1891

Alma J. Little App

- Born in 1867, Newton, Ohio
- Died (No records found; according to her alma mater, Oberlin College, she had "chronic unknown whereabouts")
- Married Harvey S. App in 1895
- Divorced 1908

Celia Ashmun Baker

- Born in 1851, Hudson, Ohio
- Died in 1896, Denver, Colorado
- Married Dr. George Griswold Baker in 1873
- Had four children, Charles, Fred, George, and Kate

Lucy Ione Edgerton

- Born in 1867, Akron, Ohio
- Died in 1906, Akron, Ohio
- Never married

Sybil A. Caskey Fair

- Born in 1861, Johnson's Corners (Barberton), Ohio
- Died in 1941, Cleveland, Ohio
- Married Dr. William C. Fair, a veterinarian, in 1894
- Had two daughters, Gladys and Mildred

Martha Herrold Fitzpatrick

- Born about 1860, Pennsylvania
- Died in 1948, Philadelphia, Pennsylvania
- Married Charles H. Christie of Cleveland in 1891
- Husband judged insane, 1900
- Married John A. Fitzpatrick of Philadelphia in 1910

Sarah E. Motz McCrum

- Born in 1865, Altoona, Pennsylvania
- Died in 1933, Buenos Aires, Argentina
- Married John Homer McCrum in 1891
- Had three children, Ralph, Helen, and Harold

Harriet "Hattie" M. Seiberling Miles

- Born in 1865, probably in Akron, Ohio
- Died in 1936, San Diego, California
- Married Lucius C. Miles in 1887

Jessie L. Wolfe Otis

- Born in 1865, Lewisburg, Ohio
- Died in 1919, in Akron, Ohio
- Married Edward P. Otis in 1887
- Had one daughter, Katherine

Zelle Adams Oviatt

- Born in 1867, probably in Akron, Ohio
- Died in 1943, Santa Barbara, California
- Married Edward Oviatt in 1891
- Had one son, Tod

Lillie May Burnham Saunders

- Born in 1857, Akron, Ohio
- Died in 1926, Akron, Ohio
- Married Addison T. Saunders in 1881

Opposite, clockwise from top: From the *Akron Daily Democrat*, November 11, 1902; From the *Piqua Daily Call*, November 11, 1902

NO NIGHT CONCERTS.

Tuesday Musical Club Has Canceled Every Engagement.

There will be no evening course of concerts under the Tuesday Musical club's auspices this season, and the existence of the club itself is threatened. Year by year the sale of tickets for the Tuesday club's course has decreased, though the quality and cost of the talent presented has increased, rather than grown less. This year the sale of tickets has been but one-third what it should have been and the club has decided that it would be unwise to go ahead with the concerts and incur a financial obligation which it would not be able to meet. The course was to have opened with the appearance of the Pittsburg orchestra next week. Now every evening concert has been canceled.

The afternoon section of the club may and probably will be continued. A decision has not been reached. The mixed chorus will be disbanded. It may be that another season the club will resume its evening concerts. This will depend upon the encouragement received when the time comes.

MUSICAL CLUB IS BANKRUPT

Akron, O., Nov. 11—The Tuesday Musical Club, an organization composed of the society people of this city and which has been in existence for the post 15 years, has filed a petition in volutary bankruptcy. The liabilities are $1,500 and the assets nothing.

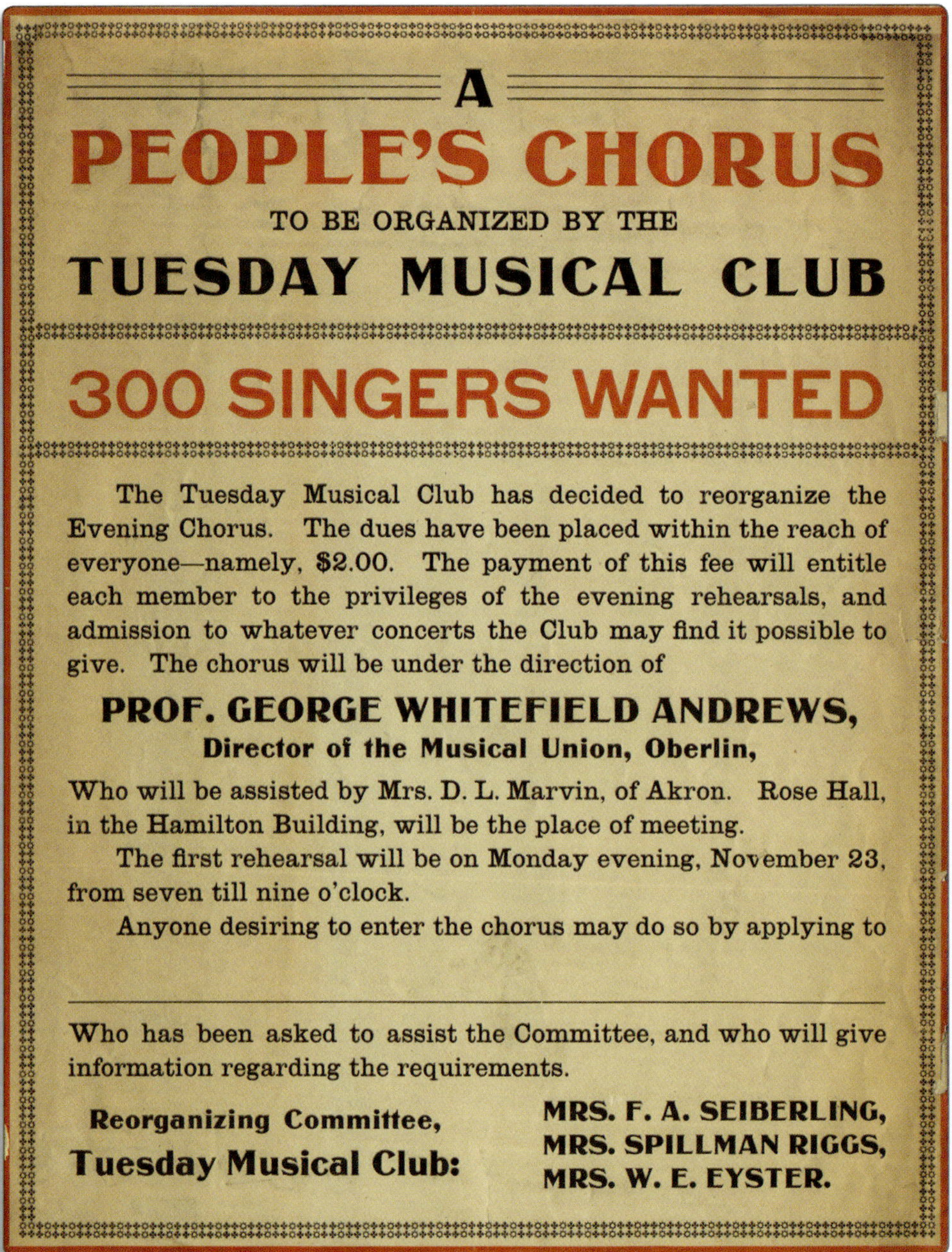

A

PEOPLE'S CHORUS

TO BE ORGANIZED BY THE

TUESDAY MUSICAL CLUB

300 SINGERS WANTED

The Tuesday Musical Club has decided to reorganize the Evening Chorus. The dues have been placed within the reach of everyone—namely, $2.00. The payment of this fee will entitle each member to the privileges of the evening rehearsals, and admission to whatever concerts the Club may find it possible to give. The chorus will be under the direction of

PROF. GEORGE WHITEFIELD ANDREWS,
Director of the Musical Union, Oberlin,

Who will be assisted by Mrs. D. L. Marvin, of Akron. Rose Hall, in the Hamilton Building, will be the place of meeting.

The first rehearsal will be on Monday evening, November 23, from seven till nine o'clock.

Anyone desiring to enter the chorus may do so by applying to

Who has been asked to assist the Committee, and who will give information regarding the requirements.

Reorganizing Committee,
Tuesday Musical Club:

MRS. F. A. SEIBERLING,
MRS. SPILLMAN RIGGS,
MRS. W. E. EYSTER.

Poster circa 1903, source unknown

A New Home for the New Century, 1904–1918

GERTRUDE SEIBERLING'S publicity efforts and the People's Chorus were a success, partly due to the construction of the German-American Music Hall, a space the club was able to use for meetings and performances. Situated at the corner of Exchange and High Streets, where the *Akron Beacon Journal* building now stands, the imposing Tudor-style hall boasted a seating capacity of up to two thousand and a stage large enough to hold eight hundred. August Miller built the hall for the German-American Company with the express purpose of accommodating Tuesday Musical and other Akron musical societies, like the Liedertafel. Tuesday Musical's first season in the hall ended on a high note, with a small surplus in their coffers and renewed hope for the future.

However, their ambitions soon outreached their reorganized abilities. By 1905, the group was once again on the brink of bankruptcy, with a projected deficit of a thousand dollars. Local newspapers ran competing headlines for and against a public campaign to shore up

Tuesday Musical members are in fine dress for this group portrait, circa 1917

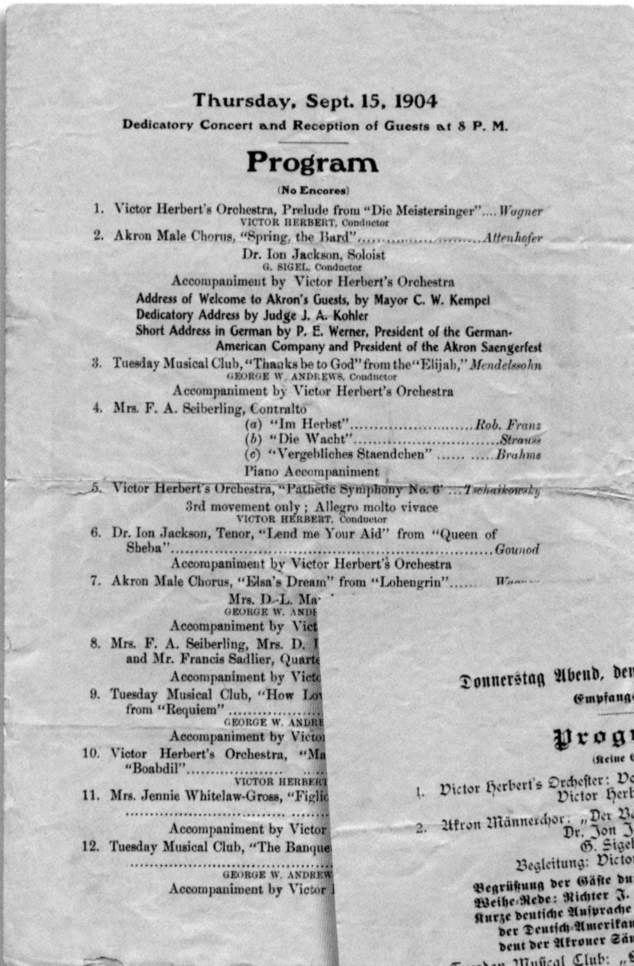

Thursday, Sept. 15, 1904

Dedicatory Concert and Reception of Guests at 8 P. M.

Program

(No Encores)

1. Victor Herbert's Orchestra, Prelude from "Die Meistersinger"....*Wagner*
VICTOR HERBERT, Conductor
2. Akron Male Chorus, "Spring, the Bard"........................*Attenhofer*
Dr. Ion Jackson, Soloist
G. SIGEL, Conductor
Accompaniment by Victor Herbert's Orchestra

Address of Welcome to Akron's Guests, by Mayor C. W. Kempel
Dedicatory Address by Judge J. A. Kohler
Short Address in German by P. E. Werner, President of the German-American Company and President of the Akron Saengerfest

3. Tuesday Musical Club, "Thanks be to God" from the "Elijah," *Mendelssohn*
GEORGE W. ANDREWS, Conductor
Accompaniment by Victor Herbert's Orchestra
4. Mrs. F. A. Seiberling, Contralto
(*a*) "Im Herbst"........................*Rob. Franz*
(*b*) "Die Wacht"............................*Strauss*
(*c*) "Vergebliches Staendchen" ....*Brahms*
Piano Accompaniment
5. Victor Herbert's Orchestra, "Pathetic Symphony No. 6" ...*Tschaikowsky*
3rd movement only ; Allegro molto vivace
VICTOR HERBERT, Conductor
6. Dr. Ion Jackson, Tenor, "Lend me Your Aid" from "Queen of Sheba"..*Gounod*
Accompaniment by Victor Herbert's Orchestra
7. Akron Male Chorus, "Elsa's Dream" from "Lohengrin"......
Mrs. D. L. Ma
GEORGE W. AND
Accompaniment by Vict
8. Mrs. F. A. Seiberling, Mrs. D. I
and Mr. Francis Sadlier, Quart
Accompaniment by Vict
9. Tuesday Musical Club, "How Lo
from "Requiem" ....
GEORGE W. ANDRE
Accompaniment by Victo
10. Victor Herbert's Orchestra, "Ma
"Boabdil"..................
VICTOR HERBER
11. Mrs. Jennie Whitelaw-Gross, "Figli
Accompaniment by Victor
12. Tuesday Musical Club, "The Banque
GEORGE W. ANDREW
Accompaniment by Victor

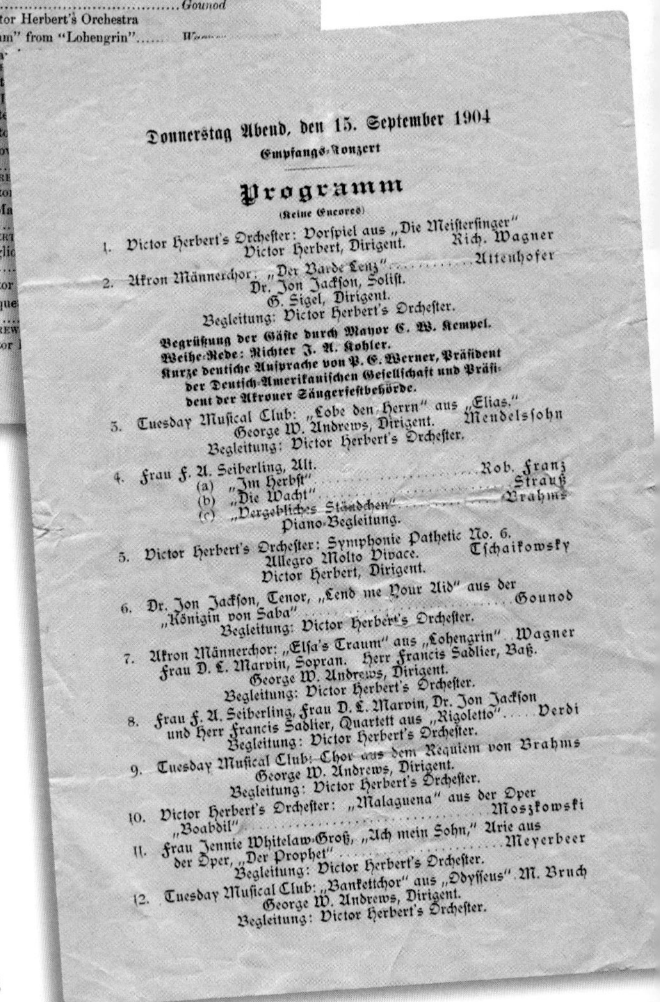

Donnerstag Abend, den 15. September 1904

Empfangs-Konzert

Programm

(Keine Encores)

1. Victor Herbert's Orchester: Vorspiel aus „Die Meistersinger" Rich. Wagner
Victor Herbert, Dirigent.
2. Akron Männerchor: „Der Barde Lenz"...........Attenhofer
Dr. Jon Jackson, Solist.
G. Sigel, Dirigent.
Begleitung: Victor Herbert's Orchester.

Begrüßung der Gäste durch Mayor C. W. Kempel.
Weihe-Rede: Richter J. A. Kohler.
Kurze deutsche Ansprache von P. E. Werner, Präsident der Deutsch-Amerikanischen Gesellschaft und Präsident der Akroner Sängerfestbehörde.

3. Tuesday Musical Club: „Lobe den Herrn" aus „Elias." Mendelssohn
George W. Andrews, Dirigent.
Begleitung: Victor Herbert's Orchester.
4. Frau F. A. Seiberling, Alt.
(a) „Im Herbst"..................Rob. Franz
(b) „Die Wacht"..................Strauß
(c) „Vergebliches Ständchen"..................Brahms
Piano-Begleitung.
5. Victor Herbert's Orchester: Symphonie Pathetic No. 6. Tschaikowsky
Allegro Molto Vivace.
Victor Herbert, Dirigent.
6. Dr. Jon Jackson, Tenor, „Lend me Your Aid" aus der „Königin von Saba"..................Gounod
Begleitung: Victor Herbert's Orchester.
7. Akron Männerchor: „Elsa's Traum" aus „Lohengrin"..Wagner
Frau D. L. Marvin, Sopran. Herr Francis Sadlier, Baß.
George W. Andrews, Dirigent.
Begleitung: Victor Herbert's Orchester.
8. Frau F. A. Seiberling, Frau D. L. Marvin, Dr. Jon Jackson und Herr Francis Sadlier, Quartett aus „Rigoletto".....Verdi
Begleitung: Victor Herbert's Orchester.
9. Tuesday Musical Club: Chor aus dem Requiem von Brahms
George W. Andrews, Dirigent.
Begleitung: Victor Herbert's Orchester.
10. Victor Herbert's Orchester: „Malaguena" aus der Oper „Boabdil"..................Moszkowski
11. Frau Jennie Whitelaw-Groß, „Ach mein Sohn," Arie aus der Oper, „Der Prophet"..................Meyerbeer
Begleitung: Victor Herbert's Orchester.
12. Tuesday Musical Club: „Bankettchor" aus „Odysseus". M. Bruch
George W. Andrews, Dirigent.
Begleitung: Victor Herbert's Orchester.

Above, clockwise from top: Program for the dedication of the German-American Music Hall in 1904, in English and German

Opposite: An illustration of the German-American Music Hall, from the dedication program, 1904

the club's shortfall, and rumors of classism in the organization put a nasty spin on the whole situation. Eventually, Tuesday Musical managed to raise the funds it needed to survive. The club also addressed the concerns of some of their critics; membership dues and concert ticket prices were lowered. These moves, as well as loosened audition standards for members, opened the club to a broader section of Akron's working population, embedded the group in the community's ethos, and reenergized the club's leadership with new, enthusiastic members. In 1906, as a testament to the club's new-found success, Tuesday Musical won the six-hundred-dollar first prize at Eisteddfod in Canton, beating out nine other competing choral groups.

During this era, Tuesday Musical developed its reputation for bringing world-class performers from far and wide to Akron. Longtime members, such as Gertrude Seiberling and Mary Zipperlen Schumacher, traveled extensively and were always on the lookout for new and intriguing talent to grace the club's stage. Gertrude Seiberling gave a noteworthy performance of her own in 1910 when she sang with tenor

H. Evan Williams—who had lately led the chorus to victory in Canton—at the Taft White House. Between 1912 and 1915, the Seiberlings undertook construction of their country estate, Stan Hywet; the music room there accommodated Tuesday Musical meetings, recitals, and guest performers for many subsequent decades. Having weathered great organizational changes and two bankruptcies in just one decade, the club wondered what the rest of the twentieth century would bring. War still raged in Europe and an 'unsinkable' ocean liner succumbed to the icy Atlantic; what challenges would be next for Tuesday Musical?

NOT DESERTED.

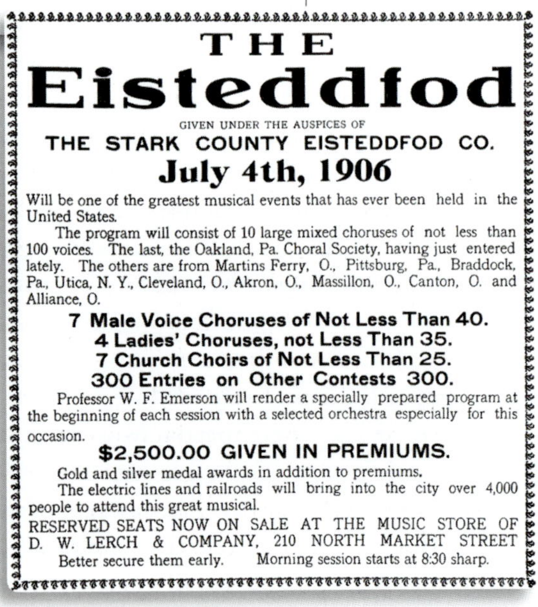
THE
Eisteddfod
GIVEN UNDER THE AUSPICES OF
THE STARK COUNTY EISTEDDFOD CO.
July 4th, 1906

Will be one of the greatest musical events that has ever been held in the United States.

The program will consist of 10 large mixed choruses of not less than 100 voices. The last, the Oakland, Pa. Choral Society, having just entered lately. The others are from Martins Ferry, O., Pittsburg, Pa., Braddock, Pa., Utica, N. Y., Cleveland, O., Akron, O., Massillon, O., Canton, O. and Alliance, O.

7 Male Voice Choruses of Not Less Than 40.
4 Ladies' Choruses, not Less Than 35.
7 Church Choirs of Not Less Than 25.
300 Entries on Other Contests 300.

Professor W. F. Emerson will render a specially prepared program at the beginning of each session with a selected orchestra especially for this occasion.

$2,500.00 GIVEN IN PREMIUMS.

Gold and silver medal awards in addition to premiums.

The electric lines and railroads will bring into the city over 4,000 people to attend this great musical.

RESERVED SEATS NOW ON SALE AT THE MUSIC STORE OF D. W. LERCH & COMPANY, 210 NORTH MARKET STREET

Better secure them early. Morning session starts at 8:30 sharp.

Above: An illustration from the *Akron Beacon Journal*, December 19, 1905; Advertisement for the Stark County Eisteddfod—Tuesday Musical's mixed chorus won first prize, from the *Stark County Democrat*, July 3, 1906

Opposite: From the *Akron Beacon Journal*, August 16, 1904

ANNIE KATHERINE MUSSER BRUOT (Katherine), younger daughter of Civil War veteran George Musser and his wife Lucetta Hughes Musser, was born on May 16, 1875, in West Salem, Ohio. During the 1880s, the family relocated to Kent, Ohio, where George became the first manager for the Atlantic and Great Western Railroad's elegant station restaurant on Franklin Street.

Nothing is known about Katherine's education. On June 19, 1895, she married Charles J. Bruot, a fellow musician seven years her senior. In 1897, the musicians lived with his parents, James F. and Rosalia Bruot, at 149 North Summit Street. The following year, Charles became a clerk at the American Cereal Company, and they moved to 123 South Maple.

The turn of the century brought much change for Katherine. In August 1899, she hosted her mother and young brother at 117 North Broadway. A month later, Charles joined the orchestra of Chase's Grand Opera House in Washington, D.C. Katherine remained in Akron, and in November she provided accompaniment for the evening festivities of the New Century Club.

Katherine's professional work continued in Akron during 1900. In February, she was the organist for the successful *Elijah, the Grand Oratorio*, presented by Tuesday Musical. That same month she and Charles were selected as the musicians for the May opening of the Lakeside Casino. The casino's successful

AKRON BECOMING A MUSICAL CENTER

Work of Tuesday Club Has Been Largely Responsible for It.

The music-loving public of Akron has great reason to be proud of the rapid strides which the city is taking in the direction of advancement and appreciation of the higher class of music and art.

With the completion of the new Music hall, Akron will rank among the foremost musical cities of the country in its facilities for producing the great modern chorus and orchestral performances. With the great organ, a masterpiece of the organ builder's art, the community will have the opportunity of hearing music, which heretofore has only been possible to a very limited degree.

With the grand work of the Tuesday Musical club under the management of its able president, Mrs. Spillman Riggs, and by whose efforts the great organ became an assured fact, in the upbuilding of the musical sentiment of Akron, all who in any way are interested in music can well sympathize, and it is by the cordial cooperation of all these that Akron can maintain the proud position to which it has attained, as a musical center, within the last decade. The course of concerts to be given this coming season by the club is one that is unsurpassed in the excellence of its general character, and the ability and reputation of the leading artists engaged. Very few persons are aware of the immense amount of detail work and concentrated effort that involves upon one in charge, and when it is considered that the untiring efforts of Mrs. Riggs and the other members of the club have been wholly a labor of love without compensatin other than the satisfactin of attending the knowledge of services well performed, it becomes a matter of pride that all shall lend their best endeavors to uphold both these disinterested workers give such support both moral and financial as shall make the coming concert season the greatest that Akron has ever known.

opening almost went on without Charles, who arrived from Washington just in time to make the engagement. The couple continued to perform at the Lakeside Casino during the summer of 1900. By December 1900, Charles was named the director of Chase's Grand Opera House.

In June 1901, Katherine sued Charles for divorce; the decree was granted in September. In October, Katherine began to offer music courses in the city at 104 North Summit Street, down the street from her former in-laws. Throughout the winter she continued to perform with Tuesday Musical and served as organist for the oratorio in early 1902.

On Christmas Day, 1903, Charles Bruot died in Akron. Katherine continued her work as a music teacher, accompanist, and performer in

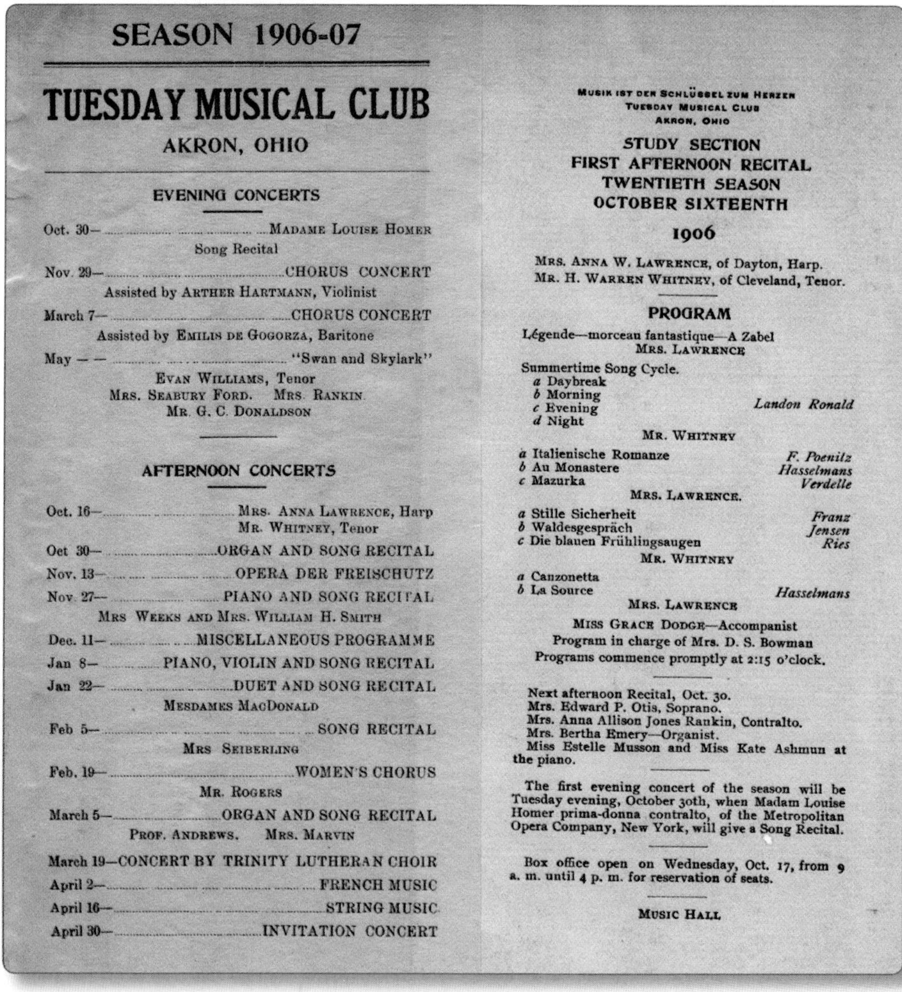

SEASON 1906-07

TUESDAY MUSICAL CLUB

AKRON, OHIO

EVENING CONCERTS

Oct. 30— .... MADAME LOUISE HOMER
Song Recital

Nov. 29— .... CHORUS CONCERT
Assisted by ARTHER HARTMANN, Violinist

March 7— .... CHORUS CONCERT
Assisted by EMILIS DE GOGORZA, Baritone

May — — .... "Swan and Skylark"
EVAN WILLIAMS, Tenor
MRS. SEABURY FORD. MRS. RANKIN.
MR. G. C. DONALDSON

AFTERNOON CONCERTS

Oct. 16— .... MRS. ANNA LAWRENCE, Harp
MR. WHITNEY, Tenor

Oct 30— .... ORGAN AND SONG RECITAL

Nov. 13— .... OPERA DER FREISCHUTZ

Nov. 27— .... PIANO AND SONG RECITAL
MRS WEEKS AND MRS. WILLIAM H. SMITH

Dec. 11— .... MISCELLANEOUS PROGRAMME

Jan 8— .... PIANO, VIOLIN AND SONG RECITAL

Jan 22— .... DUET AND SONG RECITAL
MESDAMES MACDONALD

Feb 5— .... SONG RECITAL
MRS SEIBERLING

Feb. 19— .... WOMEN'S CHORUS
MR. ROGERS

March 5— .... ORGAN AND SONG RECITAL
PROF. ANDREWS. MRS. MARVIN

March 19—CONCERT BY TRINITY LUTHERAN CHOIR

April 2— .... FRENCH MUSIC

April 16— .... STRING MUSIC

April 30— .... INVITATION CONCERT

MUSIK IST DER SCHLÜSSEL ZUM HERZEN
TUESDAY MUSICAL CLUB
AKRON, OHIO

STUDY SECTION
FIRST AFTERNOON RECITAL
TWENTIETH SEASON
OCTOBER SIXTEENTH

1906

MRS. ANNA W. LAWRENCE, of Dayton, Harp.
MR. H. WARREN WHITNEY, of Cleveland, Tenor.

PROGRAM

Légende—morceau fantastique—A Zabel
MRS. LAWRENCE

Summertime Song Cycle.
a Daybreak
b Morning
c Evening — *Landon Ronald*
d Night
MR. WHITNEY

a Italienische Romanze — *F. Poenitz*
b Au Monastere — *Hasselmans*
c Mazurka — *Verdelle*
MRS. LAWRENCE.

a Stille Sicherheit — *Franz*
b Waldesgespräch — *Jensen*
c Die blauen Frühlingsaugen — *Ries*
MR. WHITNEY

a Canzonetta
b La Source — *Hasselmans*
MRS. LAWRENCE

MISS GRACE DODGE—Accompanist
Program in charge of Mrs. D. S. Bowman
Programs commence promptly at 2:15 o'clock.

Next afternoon Recital, Oct. 30.
Mrs. Edward P. Otis, Soprano.
Mrs. Anna Allison Jones Rankin, Contralto.
Mrs. Bertha Emery—Organist.
Miss Estelle Musson and Miss Kate Ashmun at the piano.

The first evening concert of the season will be Tuesday evening, October 30th, when Madam Louise Homer prima-donna contralto, of the Metropolitan Opera Company, New York, will give a Song Recital.

Box office open on Wednesday, Oct. 17, from 9 a. m. until 4 p. m. for reservation of seats.

MUSIC HALL

the area. On December 16, 1910, she accompanied her neighbor, Welsh tenor H. Evan Williams, and fellow club member, Gertrude Seiberling, during their performance at the White House.

Continuing her affiliation with the club, Katherine became its president in 1910. In September 1915, she was hired at the Strand Theatre, 113 South Main Street. Each day at this opulent $225,000 motion picture theater located between Mill and Bowery Streets, Katherine provided the music for the movies.

By 1920, Katherine was listed in *Groves' Dictionary of Music and Musicians, the American Supplement* as president of the State Music Teachers' Association, with a contact address of 70 North Prospect in Akron. She also was listed as a music instructor in the 1925–26 catalog of the Municipal University of Akron and continued to live at 715 West Market Street for decades. She died January 23, 1967, in an Akron long-term care facility.

First Concert
October twenty-sixth

Mlle. Jeanne Gerville-Reache

Prima Dona Contralto

from the Manhattan Opera House
New York

Jeanne Gerville-Reache, who has been acclaimed as the finest contralto heard on the stage since Alboni, is a Frenchwoman but of Spanish blood as well, for her mother is a Spaniard. From her the the young singer inherits her lustrous black eyes, her jet black hair, and a certain languorous grace thoroughly Andalusian. Yet she is French by training and education.

Gerville-Reache has been chosen as the star soloist on Artists' night at the Worchester Festival. She won brilliant triumphs at the Opera Comique Paris, Theatre de la Monnaie-Brussels and Convent Garden, London. She owes her wonderful popularity in concert work to the remarkable beauty and purity of her voice, her impeccable technique, and her radiant personality.

Opposite: From the 1906–07 season announcement
Above: From the 1909–10 season announcement

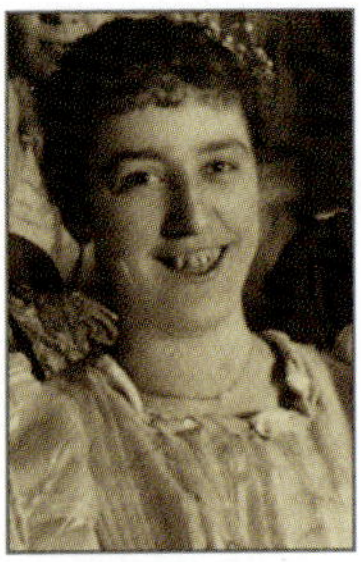

MINNE ETTA (MINNETTA) HENEBERGER RIGGS, along with Elizabeth Eyster and Gertrude Seiberling, undertook the reorganization of the club in late 1903. The surviving twin daughter of Wesley and Mary Hershey was born on December 6, 1870, in Wayne County, Ohio.

As a teen, Minne Etta suffered a foot injury which necessitated several surgeries and left her an invalid for several years. While this might have deterred others, she met the challenge of studying organ at Oberlin College, noting that many never detected her adaptive measures to master pedaling techniques. Minne Etta's abilities led her to study with French composer and organist Félix-Alexandre Guilmant. Among his other students at that time were future composer and teacher Nadia Boulanger and organist-composer Marcel Dupré.

Minne Etta became well-recognized by the Akron community for her work as the manager of the successful star entertainment lecture series. Her fund-raising efforts included a recital in May 1901, which garnered a thousand dollars for the German-American Music Hall. In August of that year she accepted the challenge of raising ten thousand dollars for the hall's new pipe organ.

Her dedication to her music and her work balanced the events of her personal life. Early in 1901, her mother died; later that year, she traveled to Indiana to nurse her ailing younger brother, George. He managed the Central Lyceum series in Indiana for their uncle, Reverend S. B. Hershey of Rochester. George succumbed to typhoid in mid-October. Two weeks after his death, Minne Etta celebrated her nuptials to H. Spillman Riggs, the noted Columbus humorist and lecturer, who managed the Central Lyceum's interests in Ohio and West Virginia.

Minne Etta assumed the duties of club president during the 1903 reorganization. With the help of Elizabeth Eyster and Gertrude Seiberling, she sought to strengthen the organiza-

Above: Tickets from the 1909–10 season

Opposite: From the *Akron Beacon Journal*, September 21, 1912 tion through expanded chorus participation and membership. Minne Etta's efforts also helped the club secure a larger, more dedicated space for public concerts; the concerts would become a source of sustaining revenue for the club. By August 1904, just prior to the opening of the new music hall, she coordinated the installation of the new organ.

TUESDAY MUSICAL CLUB PLANS GREAT THINGS DURING ITS TWENTY FIFTH YEAR

Concerts Will be Best Ever Given—Men's Chorus Will be Formed and Concert by Men is Also Planned—Club Work Has Started With a Vim.

This is the 25th anniversary of the Tuesday Musical club and every effort is being made to make this club chorus the biggest and best ever. The standard of the club has been set very high and must be successfully maintained. Nature is full of music, why not get our minds and hearts full of it, also? Music is educational, uplifting and it is the art which appeals most powerfully to the individual and is so readily felt that we do not attach importance enough to it. The true inward nature of music, the scientist and philosopher has not yet discovered.

Akron is a very enterprising city and not only is it essential for its business interests to increase, but its art and literature must keep pace and the loyal Akron people must give these things their consideration. The musical atmosphere created by the Tuesday Musical club is healthful and exhilirating and it is esteemed a great pleasure to belong to this chorus which has had years of efficient training. Dr. O H. Evans of Marysville is the very able director for the year. Do Akron people, as a rule realize the wonderful work the musical clubs of the city are accomplishing? Young men and women are given the society and benefit of conservatory trained musicians. The unselfishness and philosophical attitude of these trained singers, for the love of the work, 'is noteworthy. There is no money gain to be considered, for there is none. The chorus members are entitled to one afternoon and one evening ticket, 14 concerts in all, gratis.

There is a great desire on the part of the managers of the club to form a men's chorus this Winter, and all men with good voices and some knowledge of music, are invited to enter. There will be two public appearances of the chorus this season. In December a miscellaneous program will be given, with the club chorus and local artists, and in February a concert with Evans Williams as soloist. This will be the tenor's only appearance in the city this Winter.

The artists' concert of the course will be given November 27 by the Cincinnati Orchestra, and on April 1 the world renowned Godomsky will give a program of piano music. He is in such demand in the United States that his manager after booking him was obliged to make a special arrangement with him for 20 additional concerts. The club meets every Monday evening at 7:30 in Neighborhood House on High street, in easy access to both East Market and Loop line cars.

Due to Spillman's continued success on the lecture circuit, the Riggs relocated to Chicago in late 1906 or early 1907. Minne Etta was preparing to perform a series of organ recitals there when her foot ailments reoccurred. By June 22, after five operations to remove tubercular growths, her left foot was amputated. Later that year more tuberculosis was discovered and the limb was further amputated. Minne Etta's surgeon scheduled a third amputation for January 5, 1908, but she and Spillman chose alternative Christian Scientist treatments. Minne Etta later wrote a testimony, describing her rapid healing; within months of her first treatment, she was able to walk with an artificial foot. She resumed her musical career, playing for multiple Sunday services in August 1908. Spillman died within a few years of her recovery.

As a result of her personal experiences, Minne Etta became a Christian Scientist practitioner. While she remarried approximately ten years after Spillman's death, the relationship ended in divorce. There were no further mentions of her musical career. Minne Etta died September 26, 1946 in Chicago, Illinois.

GERTRUDE PENFIELD SEIBERLING was an honorary president of Tuesday Musical. The youngest daughter of Willoughby businessman James Wakeman and Elsie Ferguson Penfield, Gertrude was born January 23, 1866. Her early ties to the Akron area began at Lasell Seminary for Young Women, outside Boston. One of her classmates, Harriet Seiberling, introduced Gertrude to her brother, Franklin A. (F. A.) Seiberling. Gertrude graduated from Lasell in 1887 and on October 12, she married F. A. and settled into life in Akron. In November 1887, her friend and sister-in-law Harriet (Harriet Seiberling Miles) helped found the club.

Recognized for her contralto voice, Gertrude became a mainstay of the choral circuit in the city. During the 1890s, she not only performed in the study and concert sections of club, but also at the Academy of Music, the opera house owned by her father-in-law.

In the early 1900s, the club experienced its first serious decline. Helen Storer Collins had shifted her efforts to the National Federation of Music Clubs and longtime member, former president, and Buchtel College music teacher Katherine Seymour Parsons departed to Hartford, Connecticut. Finally, a committee of three—treasurer Elizabeth Eyster, new president Minne Etta Heneberger Riggs, and an enthusiastic Gertrude—undertook the group's redevelopment. Gertrude suggested restructuring evening concert ticket prices and broadening chorus membership requirements to ensure a broader base of city representation in the club.

Gertrude attended the 1901 biennial convention of the National Federation of Music Clubs in Cleveland. In 1913, she became state vice president of Ohio and in 1915, reorganized the Ohio Federation. Her home, Stan Hywet Hall, was the site of numerous board meetings from 1917 through the end of her term as the federation's ninth president in 1921. Her leadership spearheaded extensive development of junior memberships and courses of study. Gertrude declined a second presidency to chair the newly created department of finance. In later years she aided in music study course development.

In 1921, after her presidency of the National Federation of Music Clubs, Gertrude joined efforts with her daughter Irene Seiberling

Harrison to form the St. Cecelia Choral Society, a women-only auxiliary choral group.

In addition to her leadership activities in the music organizations, Gertrude hosted not only afternoon study sessions of the club, but also meetings, concerts, and even guest celebrities. Among the notables who passed through Stan Hywet's portals were locals Helen Jepson and James Melton, both stars of the Metropolitan Opera House, as well as international artists such as Leopold Stokowsi, Ignace Paderewski, and Rosa Ponselle. In 1910, Gertrude, along with tenor H. Evan Williams and accompanist Katherine Bruot, performed for President Howard Taft and his cabinet at the White House.

December the Fourth

Extra Concert

First Methodist Church

MISS ADELINE VOSS
Soprano

H. EVAN WILLIAMS
Tenor

Handel's "Messiah"

This great work is most representative of all the work of its class. Not in opera, nor in fact in any other form of music does one composition stand out head and shoulders above its fellows, as does this. No other oratorio has enjoyed such endearing popularity—such positive adoration.

MRS. F. A. SEIBERLING
Contralto

MR. JAMES McMAHON of Cleveland
Baritone

In 1937, Gertrude celebrated two fiftieth golden anniversaries—the celebration of her marriage to F. A. and the founding of Tuesday Musical. Her longtime affiliation with the club ended with her death on January 8, 1946; she is remembered with the Gertrude Seiberling Music Education Scholarship for college-age students.

Above: From the 1909–10 season announcement

FIRST RECITAL—October Twenty-ninth

ORIGINAL SONGS AND STORIES

BY

MRS. CARRIE JACOBS BOND

Mrs. Carrie Jacobs Bond is a woman of charming personality and wonderful artistic temperament. Her stories and songs are full of human touches, pictures of humble, happy homes, and wholesome philosophy. These she gives in a delightful, natural manner, which arouses a sympathetic response in her audience. She made her debut in London a year ago last May, singing children's songs on a program with Caruso.

Here is a woman who writes poems, sets them to music, and sings them in a manner that reveals the very acme of art.—*Elbert Hubbard.*

Carrie Jacobs Bond's success throughout the afternoon was unbounded, and brought her to a position in Chicago that she has already gained in London and New York.—*Musical Leader and Concert Goer.*

MRS. W. H. COLLINS

MRS. N. O. MATHER

April Fifteenth

Mrs. J. R. Madden	Mr. Ralph Wilson
Mrs. Seth Tuttle	Mr. Richards

Ensemble Piano Music

Under the direction of

Miss Ella Bigelow

Mrs. F. B. Curran	Mrs. C. D. Haslet
Mrs. J. E. McCanna	Miss Ethel Evans
Miss Eva Dunlap	Miss Clara Bork
Miss Anna Spicer	Miss Nellie Hanks

MRS. J. R. MADDEN

ALMA GLUCK CHARMS AKRON MUSIC LOVERS IN CONCERT

Rousing Audience Captivated by Voice and Personal Charm of American Singer Whose Tones Filled Every Corner of Big Music Hall

An audience of 2300 greeted charming Alma Gluck, soprano, in the second concert of the season given Wednesday evening at East Market academy by the Tuesday Musical club. Miss Beatrice Harrison, cellist, soloist with Miss Gluck in the joint recital was no less kindly received, her wonderful technique winning her the most cordial reception granted an instrumentalist in this city during the season.

Miss Gluck's voice and secondly her personal charm reached every individual in that large assembly, making an appeal that was felt in the general applause which followed each number. She graciously responded with three encores making her evening's repertoire an unusually long one. At the last she sang "My Laddie" by request and it was the memory of this song with its soft Scotch phrasing that patrons carried away with them to remember Alma Gluck as a whole-souled girl with a beautiful voice.

Carried Throughout Hall.

Gluck's softest pianissimo carried to the farthest corner of the big academy. Her full tones were just as sweetly rounded and unforced as those of the lower register. She sang dramatically and yet without show, as if it were the expression of her own feelings that she put into the songs she gave.

Her tones appeared to leave the vocal chords unhampered, finding their natural resonance undiminished by the muscles of the throat and tongue and floating out to delight even those in the last chairs, with the purity and fullness of each spoken word.

The group of German songs, including "Du Bist die Ruh" and "Die Forelle" by Franz Schubert; "Die Lotosblume" and "Der Sandman" by Robert Schumann and "Botschaft" by Brahms showed this clear enunciation and apparent ease, so different from the shoddy pronunciation used by most singers in the rendition of German songs. Her opening number was not listed on the program. She sang Rossini's aria from "The Barber of Seville." Her other numbers were "Peasant Song" by Rachmaninoff; "Bohemian Cradle Song" by Smetana; "Fruhlingslied" by Rubinstein; "Chanson Indoue" and "Song of the Shepherd Lehl" by Rimsky-Korsakoff; to which group she gave as an encore a delightful little song, "My Little Gray Home in the West.

Sang Cadman Song.

Her last group in the English included Cadman's song, "From the Land of the Sky Blue Water", which with "Red, Red, Rose" by Cottenet shared the popularity of this group.

Miss Harrison, accompanied by Miss Marie Smith gave as her first number, "Adagio et Allegro" by Boccherini and second, Wagner-Becker's "Walther's Preislied," from "Die Meistersinger." Both performances gave every proof of that remarkable ability for clever execution on the cello, which made her a favorite in English concert circles and is fast giving the name of Beatrice Harrison a place in musicale records here. Miss Harrison played brilliantly throughout, but her principal number was that from "Die Meistersinger." To this she was forced to respond with an encore, playing "Songs My Mother Taught Me" by D'Vorak.

"Largo," by Becker; "Oriental" by Cesar Cui and "Papillon" by Harty were her final numbers in the latter the fluttering of the butterflies and exquisite coloring and beauty of flowers in a garden, sunlight on water and all the imaginative pictures painted into Hamilton Harty's "Papillon's" were cleverly brought out by the cellist.

Credit for a part of the evening's pleasure must be accorded Wilhelm Spoor accompanist for Miss Gluck and Miss Smith, who accompanied Miss Harrison.

Above, clockwise from top: The music room at Stan Hywet Hall, taken around 1917 by Willard Seiberling, courtesy of Stan Hywet Hall and Gardens; From the *Akron Beacon Journal*, January 21, 1915

Opposite, clockwise from top: From the 1907–08 season announcement; From the 1912–13 season announcement

MRS. A. E. HEINTSELMAN,
President

MRS. W. E. EYSTER,
Treasurer

MRS. CHARLES A. CASS,
Director of Programs

LEVI J. BECHTEL,
Chairman Evening Section

MISS ELLA C. BIGELOW,
Chairman Study Section

MRS. N. O. MATHER,
Secretary Study Section

CARL K. RICHARDS,
Secretary, Evening Section

LEROY P. HOLLOWAY,
Librarian, Evening Section

MRS. F. A. SEIBERLING, Honorary President

PATRONS AND PATRONESSES

Mr. and Mrs. F. H. Adams
Mr. and Mrs. F. W. Albrecht
Mr. O. C. Barber
Mr. and Mrs. J. W. Crouse
Mr. and Mrs. Jerome Dannby
Honorable and Mrs. C. W. F. Dick
Mr. and Mrs. H. S. Firestone
Mr. and Mrs. H. A. Galt
Mr. and Mrs. H. M. Houser
Mr. and Mrs. M. Otis Hower
Mr. and Mrs. P. W. Litchfield
Mr. and Mrs. A. H. Marks
Mr. and Mrs. H. B. Manton
Mr. and Mrs. I. R. Manton
Mr. and Mrs. F. H. Mason
Mr. and Mrs. A. H. Noah
Mr. and Mrs. A. T. Paige
Mr. and Mrs. C. B. Raymond
Mr. and Mrs. F. A. Seiberling
Mr. and Mrs. C. W. Seiberling
Mr. and Mrs. G. M. Stadelman
Mr. and Mrs. N. C. Stone
Mr. and Mrs. H. Evan Williams
Mr. P. E. Werner

ADVISORY BOARD

Mr. Emil Gammeter
Mr. J. Ed Good
Mr. J. P. Hale
Mr. H. M. Houser
Mr. F. H. Mason
Mr. A. H. Noah
Mr. N. C. Stone
Mr. F. A. Seiberling
Mr. E. C. Shaw
Mr. H. B. Manton

CONCERTS

Tuesday Evening, May 6th.
Wednesday Afternoon, May 7th.
Wednesday Evening, May 7th.

CONDUCTORS
Emil Oberhoffer — Dr. O. H. Evans

SOPRANO
Luella Chilson-Ohrman

CONTRALTO
Barbara Wait

TENORS
Joseph Schenke — H. Evan Williams

BARITONE
Arthur Middleton

CELLO
Cornelius VanVliet

VIOLIN
Richard Czerwonky

HARP
Henry J. Williams

MINNEAPOLIS SYMPHONY ORCHESTRA

CHORUS OF THE TUESDAY MUSICAL CLUB

MRS. KATHERINE BRUOT, Accompanist.

Concerts begin at 8 P. M. and 2:30 P. M. No one will be admitted to the hall during the performance of any number.

Above: From the May Festival program, 1913

Five Decades of Growth, 1919–1946

WHEN THE German-American Music Hall was torn down in 1917 to accommodate the new *Akron Beacon Journal* building, Tuesday Musical relocated to the Akron Armory. Despite its lack of elegant architecture, the armory, located on the corner of High and what is now Bowery Street (formerly Quarry Street), had the largest indoor seating capacity in the city at the time. Briefly used as a temporary hospital during the 1918 influenza outbreak, the multivalent building hosted wrestling matches, union meetings, political events, and, of course, training activities for the local National Guard unit. Tuesday Musical members were longtime tenants of the space, enduring leaky roofs, noisy plumbing, and uncomfortable seats in their relentless pursuit of excellent musical entertainment. The year 1918 also marked the beginning of a

Club picnic, June 22, 1926, The Ledges, courtesy of Stan Hywet Hall and Gardens

long-term relationship between Tuesday Musical and the newly-formed Cleveland Orchestra, which, with the exception of one year, has consistently performed each season with the club.

The first half of the twentieth century presented difficult challenges for the United States, and the world, but Tuesday Musical managed to survive as it always had, by the grace and courage of its members. In 1921, Gertrude Seiberling formed the St. Cecelia Choral Society, a singing group for daughters of club members. For the fortieth anniversary of the club's founding, the ladies held a grand ball, featuring an enormous tiered cake topped by forty electric candles and surrounded by members in elaborate flower costumes. The club marked it's fiftieth anniversary in 1937, as well as the fiftieth wedding anniversary of the Seiberlings, both of which were celebrated in grand style. That same year also saw the passing of a longtime and beloved member, Mary Zipperlen Schumacher, the second wife of 'Cereal King' Ferdinand Schumacher. Mary changed the future of Tuesday Musical by bequeathing them fifty thousand dollars to offset the costs of performances. That gift, wisely managed and invested, meant the club never again had to face bankruptcy.

In 1946, the club mourned another loss when Gertrude Seiberling died. Her dedication and ingenuity had helped guide the club through five decades of growth.

Program

Second Season 1922–1923

Famous Artists Concerts

Violin Recital

by

JASCHA HEIFETZ

Akron Armory

Wednesday Evening, November 1st

Local Manager, EARLE POLING

Clockwise from top: A 1922 program cover for a concert in the Famous Artists Concerts Series; From the *Akron Beacon Journal*, May 16, 1928, the ball celebrating the fortieth anniversary of Tuesday Musical, courtesy of Stan Hywet Hall and Gardens

Mammoth Birthday Cake Unveiled At Ball Sponsored By Music Club

—By Louvre Inc.

Unveiling of a great birthday cake was one of the principal features of the ball which the Tuesday Musical club gave at East Market Gardens on Tuesday to celebrate the 40th anniversary of its founding. The cake was a mammoth tiered affair of white with 40 tall pink candles topped by electric lights. Before its unveiling it was surrounded by a diaphanous circular curtain. Around the bottom layer of the cake were grouped 40 club members in pink and white costumes. When the curtain was lifted they left their places and gave a song and parade specialty that was one of the loveliest things of the entire ball.

Members who represented candles in the cake were:

Mrs. Claire App, Mrs. A. J. Akers, Mrs. E. S. Babcox, Mrs. Katherine Bruot, Mrs. Lester W. Brock, Mrs. Charles C. Baird, Mrs. J. S. Baer, Mrs. Julia Croft, Mrs. M. T. Christy, Mrs. E. H. Clinedinst, Mrs. L. C. McGinley, Mrs. Frank W. Fox, Mrs. Robert Guinther, Mrs G. B. Lovett, Miss Gertrude Miller, Mrs Carl K. Richards, Mrs. Marie Van Rennes, Miss Katherine Reed, Mrs. Frank Starbird, Mrs. R. W. Shumacher, Mrs. Arthur Sidwell, Mrs. Ed Scheck, Miss Katherine McMillen, Mrs. Jan Teppema, Mrs. Walter Irwin, Mrs. D. K. Paige, Mrs. F. S. Goehring, Mrs. R. F. Thaw, Miss Ruth Porter, Mrs. H. T. Metcalf, Mrs. C. W. Lonsbury, Mrs J. H. Shreffler, Miss Gertrude Pettijohn, Mrs. John Shosenberg, Mrs. W. H. Zorn, Mrs. E. E. Crites, Mrs. A. E. Chandler, Mrs. T. A Rees, Mrs E. R. Case and Mrs. D. O. Webster.

Opposite: Gertrude Seiberling (middle, front row) and a group of prominent women in the National Federation of Music Clubs. Taken in 1921, on the West Terrace of Stan Hywet Hall by Bachrach, courtesy of Stan Hywet Hall and Gardens

EFFIE D. METCALF BOWMAN was born on November 6, 1867, in McConnelsville, Morgan County, Ohio. Nothing is known about her life prior to her November 8, 1893 marriage to Dr. Dell Scotland Bowman in Morgan County.

In 1894, the Bowmans resided at 151 Crosby Street, Akron. By 1900, Effie's younger sister Nellie had joined them. In 1903, the Bowmans moved to 339 Crosby, combining their home and the doctor's practice at one location. Effie was elected treasurer of the club that same year.

Three years later, the Bowmans welcomed their daughter, Jean, on March 11, 1906. Almost exactly a year later—following the resignation of the club president, Mrs. C. E. House—Effie was elected president in an emergency meeting. Effie guided the club through the following year, but indicated she would not accept another term as president, citing her own ill health due to "overwork and nervous strain," which would require three months of bed rest.

Perhaps some of the overwork in 1909 was caused by the organization of a new household at 345 Crosby Street, where the 1910 and 1920 censuses found the Bowmans. In 1921, Effie was elected president again; she would continue in the position for the next fifteen years, with essentially the same executive board. During Effie's leadership, the club sponsored discounted evening concert seats for the working class, and an opera study division, led by Gertrude Seiberling, was formed. Effie presided over both the fortieth and fiftieth anniversary celebrations of the club, assisting in the organization of talent and concerts, which steadily increased the reputation of the club in the area.

Dr. Dell Bowman died on April 18, 1943; Effie died December 15, 1945.

Tuesday Musical Club

EVENING CONCERT COURSE
SEASON 1929-30

THE AMERICAN OPERA CO.
NOVEMBER 7
AT GOODYEAR THEATRE

DETROIT SYMPHONY ORCHESTRA
NOVEMBER 14
AT AKRON ARMORY

HOROWITZ, Pianist
NOVEMBER 19
AT AKRON ARMORY

CLEVELAND SYMPHONY ORCHESTRA
MARCH 4
AT AKRON ARMORY

SIGRID ONEGIN, Contralto
APRIL 1
AT AKRON ARMORY

Reservations for patron tickets may be made by mail or telephone to the President of the Club, Mrs. D. S. Bowman, 345 Crosby St. Lincoln 1942.

will open Wednesday, Sept. 25th, at 9

From the 1929–30 season announcement

MARY E. ZIPPERLEN SCHUMACHER, was born November 28, 1859, in Clinton, Ohio, the youngest daughter of Civil War surgeon Dr. Adolf Zipperlen and his wife Marie, immigrants from Germany. After Dr. Zipperlen left the 108th Regular Ohio Volunteer Infantry in 1865, the family relocated to Cincinnati. The 1880 U.S. Census lists twenty-year-old Mary as a public school teacher living at 23 Webster Street, the Zipperlen home.

Having made friends and contacts among the many Germans who relocated to Ohio during the years of Germany's unification, the Zipperlens were well-acquainted with Ferdinand Schumacher of Akron and his wife Hermine. Ferdinand, the 'Cereal King,' had immigrated from Celle, Hanover, Germany. By 1856, he was involved in the production of cereal products in Akron. In 1891, the F. Schumacher Milling Company consolidated with the American Cereal Company and Ferdinand was named president. On June 1, 1893, Hermine Schumacher died.

Mary Zipperlen's marriage to Ferdinand on August 1, 1899, in San Francisco, California, was a surprise to both friends and family. The couple, who had known each other for many years, received congratulations from his friends in Akron and her family in Cincinnati. In response to their age difference and the spontaneity of their marriage, Mary described the ceremony in the August 7, 1899, *Akron Daily Democrat* as "'perfectly lovely.'" She was also quoted as having said, "'I never promised to obey.'"

The Schumachers returned to Akron in May 1900. On March 28, 1902, Mary hosted a luncheon and dinner festivities in honor of Ferdinand's eightieth birthday. This public display contrasted with their regular life of horticulture, literature, and music. During this time, Mary was active in Tuesday Musical and other clubs.

Ferdinand Schumacher died April 15, 1908. By 1920, Mary lived with her widowed sister Hermine Hanson. Her wide-ranging travels brought global musical talent and organizations to the club's attention.

In 1927, Mary presented a talk at the biennial meeting of the National Federation of Music Clubs. Her support of the club continued beyond her death on September 10, 1936, as her will designated the club as a beneficiary of her estate. Through wise investment, this bequest has funded scholarships and helped secure the future of the club.

ST. CECILIA CLUB TO GIVE OPERETTA AT STAN HYWET

—Photo by Goddard.

Left to right, back row: Mesdames Harold Graves, Edgar Williams, Lew Wallace, Sterling Alderfer, Kenneth Parke, Wilford Holcomb, Ernest Schwan, Victor Montenyohl, H. W. Delzell, Donald Gottwald, Miss Frances Kerch, Mesdames Lisle Buckingham, John Tuttle and Howard Campbell.

Front row, Mesdames Karl Meisner, Owen Roderick, Richard Brouse, Paul Tobin, John Christy, Elmer Palmer, Fred Rankin, William Foltz and Ralph W. Brightman.

Executive Board

MRS. F. A. SEIBERLING—*Honorary President*

MRS. D. S. BOWMAN.......................................*President*

MRS. CHARLES BAIRD.......................*First Vice President*

MRS. FRANK STARBIRD.................*Second Vice President*

MRS. M. T. CHRISTY.......................................*Secretary*

MRS. LESTER W. BROCK.................................*Treasurer*

MRS. J. G. STOLLER
MRS. THOMAS CASEY.....................................*Assistants*

MRS. FERDINAND SCHUMACHER........................*Historian*

MRS. E. C. DIETZ.........*Chairman Study Section Meetings*

MRS. E. E. CRITES....*Director of Study Section Programs*

MRS. R. F. THAW..*Assistant*

MRS. L. M. BUCKINGHAM..............................*Civic Music*

MRS. REXFORD BABB.................................*Junior Work*

MRS. W. P. KEITH..*Assistant*

MRS. ROBERT GUINTHER.....................*Concert Publicity*

MRS. E. S. SHECK..*Assistant*

Above, clockwise from top: From the *Akron Beacon Journal*, March 31, 1930; From the 1929 Yearbook. Apparently used to plan a meeting, with penciled-in phone numbers and acceptances

TUESDAY MUSICAL CLUB

Evening Concerts

46th SEASON - 1933 - 1934

AKRON ARMORY

3.

Josef and Rosina Lhevinne

Two Piano Recital

Tuesday Evening, February 13th, 1934

4.

Maria Olszewska

Primadonna Contralto

Metropolitan Opera

Tuesday Evening, April 10, 1934

Tickets on sale at The B. F.

Tuesday Musical Office Phon

An Afternoon Musical will be given at

Tuesday Musical Club Janua

Open to the Public

MRS. D. S. BOWMAN, President Tuesday Mu

WEDDING BY LANT

COMIC OPE

BY JEAN JACQUES (

Peter, the young owner of a large farm, has tal
Lise, at his uncle's request. Lischen is secretly
uncle's advice. Peter asks a loan from his unc
treasure and tells him to be under the old oak
bells ring, when he will find his treasure. Lis
from her old uncle. Two old village widows,
heard of the treasure which is to belong to Pet
Lischen, for the fun of it, seats herself beneath
her lover. Peter, likewise, strolls there to dig f
who fell asleep on the bench, fiinds his uncle's
in Lischen the treasurer his uncle had promise

S. HUROK

presents

Second American Tour

1933-34

VIENNA CHOIR BOYS

(WIENER SAENGERKNABEN)

Founded By
Imperial Decree
in 1498

AKRON ARMORY

Tuesday Evening, JANUARY 2nd, at 8:15

Tickets on sale at The Harbaugh Piano Co.

Tuesday Musical Club Course:

Kreisler Nov. 21. Vienna Choir Boys Jan. 2. J. & R. Lhevinne Feb. 13
Olszewska Apr. 10th

Above, clockwise from top: From the 1933–34 season announcement; The 1934 program cover for the Vienna Choir Boys concert

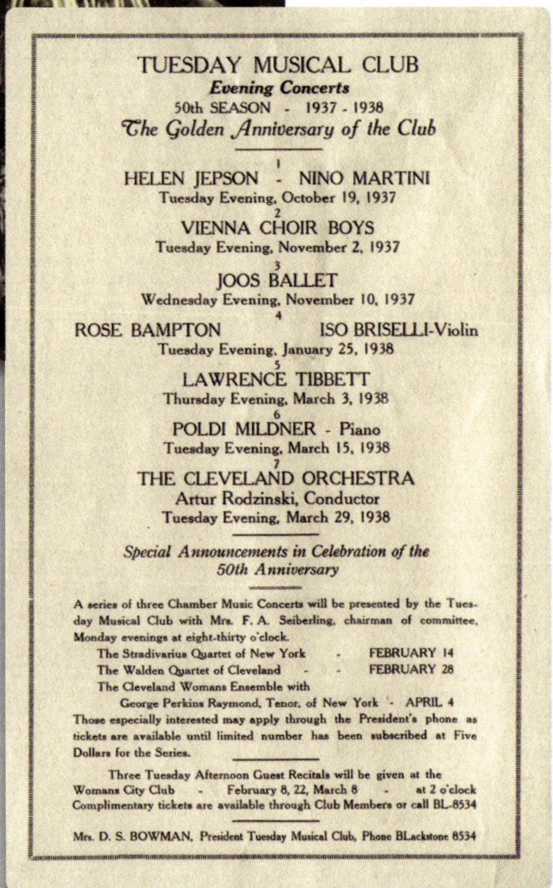

TUESDAY MUSICAL CLUB

Evening Concerts

50th SEASON - 1937 - 1938

The Golden Anniversary of the Club

1
HELEN JEPSON - NINO MARTINI
Tuesday Evening, October 19, 1937

2
VIENNA CHOIR BOYS
Tuesday Evening, November 2, 1937

3
JOOS BALLET
Wednesday Evening, November 10, 1937

4
ROSE BAMPTON ISO BRISELLI-Violin
Tuesday Evening, January 25, 1938

5
LAWRENCE TIBBETT
Thursday Evening, March 3, 1938

6
POLDI MILDNER - Piano
Tuesday Evening, March 15, 1938

7
THE CLEVELAND ORCHESTRA
Artur Rodzinski, Conductor
Tuesday Evening, March 29, 1938

Special Announcements in Celebration of the 50th Anniversary

A series of three Chamber Music Concerts will be presented by the Tuesday Musical Club with Mrs. F. A. Seiberling, chairman of committee, Monday evenings at eight-thirty o'clock.

The Stradivarius Quartet of New York - FEBRUARY 14
The Walden Quartet of Cleveland - - FEBRUARY 28
The Cleveland Womans Ensemble with
George Perkins Raymond, Tenor, of New York - APRIL 4

Those especially interested may apply through the President's phone as tickets are available until limited number has been subscribed at Five Dollars for the Series.

Three Tuesday Afternoon Guest Recitals will be given at the Womans City Club - February 8, 22, March 8 - at 2 o'clock
Complimentary tickets are available through Club Members or call BL-8534

Mrs. D. S. BOWMAN, President Tuesday Musical Club, Phone BLackstone 8534

Above, clockwise from top: A portrait of Gertrude Seiberling inscribed "Celebration of the Fiftieth Anniversary of Tuesday Musical Club 1887–1937;" A fiftieth anniversary season program, 1937–38

Opposite, clockwise from top: From the *Akron Beacon Journal*, September, 23, 1942; Invitation for the twentieth anniversary celebration of St. Cecelia's Choral Society, 1941

Wartime Brings Changes To Tuesday Musical Club Meeting

MISS SPAGHT MRS. BOWMAN MRS. STINCHCOMB MRS. STEWART MRS. OHRT

Wartime restrictions and limitations were certainly reflected on a heretofore unaffected group yesterday when Tuesday Musical club members arrived at Stan-Hywet Hall, home of Mr. and Mrs. F. A. Seiberling, with their luncheons under their arms. Because of sugar, coffee and tire rationing, the crowd presented a vastly different picture from the usual assembly that enters the heavily carved front doors. Thermos bottles, little bags of sugar, baskets of food and cretonne-covered picnic dishes were much in evidence. Mrs. Frank Manchester bicycled from her Kenilworth dr. home, picnic basket on the back seat. Among the many others attending this, the first campaign meeting of the fall ticket campaign for the club's annual concert course, were Mrs. O. G. Stinchcomb, Mrs. Brice Bowman, Miss Jeanette Spaght, campaign chairman; Mrs. Donald B. Stewart and Mrs. Henry N. Ohrt.

MRS. MANCHESTER

The Saint Cecilia Choral Society
Request the Pleasure of your Company at their
Twentieth Anniversary Celebration
on Monday the First of December, 1941
6:30 P. M. at the
Portage Country Club
$1.70 per person

Reply by November 28th, to Mrs. John M. Linforth
856 Mayfair Road, Akron, Ohio

THE TRAPP FAMILY SINGERS

SOPRANOS
Johanna von Trapp
Agatha von Trapp

MEZZO SOPRANOS
Maria van Trapp
Martina von Trapp

CONTRALTOS
Hedwig von Trapp
Baroness Maria von Trapp

TENOR
Werner von Trapp

BASS
Dr. Rupert von Trapp

Dr. Franz Wasner, *Conductor*

PROGRAM

I

Quem vidistis pastores - - *Richard Dering* (17th century)

"Whom have ye seen, O shepherds?" — "We have seen the Son of God and heard the angelic host praising His name. Alleluia!"

Ave Maria - - - *Tomas Luis de Vittoria* (16th century)

Kyrie and Agnus Dei, from Missa Brevis - *Palestrina*

Palestrina's Missa Brevis appeared in the First Book of Masses, published in 1570, and dedicated to King Philip II of Spain. The *Kyrie* is written in four parts, the *Agnus Dei* in five parts, the two soprano voices being composed as a Canon.

II

Tanzen und Springen - - *Hans Le*
(15

A joyous 5-part Ballet in praise of "dancing an

Song of Parting (Medieval folk-song) -
- - - *Arr. by Johanne*

Nachtwache (Night Watch) - - *Johanne*

The watchman's horn sounds through the nig
through the silent streets. Put out thy lamp,
soul, and lay thee down to rest.

Swedish Dance Carol - *Arr. by Katherine*

III

Trio Sonata in F, for two alto Recorders and basso continuo (viola da gamba and spinet) - - - - - - - *Georg Phillip Telemann* (18th Century)

Affettuoso
Allegro
Adagio
Allegro vivace

Sonata con arie, for Recorders, Viola da gamba, and Spinet - - *Johann Heinrich Schmelzer* (17th century)

Sonatina - Aria - Campanella - Lamento - Sonatina

From Heaven high I came to earth - *Old Christmas Carol*

Setting for Verse 1 .... *Adam Gumpeltzhaimer* (1559-1625)
" " " 2, 3 (in Christmas Oratorio) .... *J. S. Bach* (1685-1750)
" " " 4 .... *Johannes Crueger* (1598-1662)

INTERMISSION

IV

Wia mei' Diandle, mei' kloans - *Carinthian Folk-Song*

Die Aeuglan voll Wasser - A Farewell Song from Carinthia

Der spaete Abend - - - *Tyrolean Song*

V

CAROLS

Shepherds, shake off your drowsy sleep (French) - - - - - - *Arr. by Franz Wasner*

All in the morning (English) - - - - - - - - - *Arr. by R. Vaughan-Williams*

La Canzone di natale (Italian) - *Setting by Franz Wasner*

Angels we have heard on high (French) - - - - - - *Setting by Franz Wasner*

Tickets on sale at the M. O'Neil Co.
Tuesday Musical Club Box Office on 6th Floor
Club Telephone — BLackstone 1815
Mrs. D. S. Bowman, President Tuesday Musical Club - BL-8534

Above: The program from the 1942 Trapp Family Singers performance, courtesy of Stan Hywet Hall and Gardens

Tuesday Musical Club Concerts

Seven Evening Concerts at Akron Armory for

57th SEASON — 1944 - 1945

Present the following celebrated musical attractions:

1.

HELEN JEPSON, *Soprano

JAMES MELTON, *Tenor

TUESDAY EVENING, OCTOBER 24th, 1944

PATRICE MUNSEL, *Coloratura Soprano

2.

TUESDAY EVENING, NOVEMBER 21st, 1944

3.

THE BOSTON SYMPHONY ORCHESTRA

Serge Koussevitzky, *Conductor*

WEDNESDAY EVENING, DECEMBER 6th, 1944

4.

RAYA GARBOUSOVA, *Violoncello*

Flutist Accompanist

Stanley Fletcher, *Piano*

TUESDAY EVENING, JANUARY 23rd, 1945

5.

THE CLEVELAND ORCHESTRA

Vladimir Golschmann, *Guest Conductor*

TUESDAY EVENING, FEBRUARY 20th, 1945

6.

METROPOLITAN OPERA ENSEMBLE

(In costume)

***Jarmila Novotna, *Soprano;* *Hertha Glaz, Con**

Raoul Jobin, *Tenor;* *Martial Singher, *Bass-Bar.

TUESDAY EVENING, MARCH 6th, 1945

7.

THE CLEVELAND ORCHESTRA

Vladimir Golschmann, *Guest Conductor*

TUESDAY EVENING, APRIL 3rd, 1945

*Indicates members of Metropolitan Opera.

Tickets on sale at The M. O'Neil Co.

6

Clockwise from top: Pages from the 1944–45 season announcement; A memorial to Gertrude Seiberling from a Seiberling Singers program, 1946, courtesy of Stan Hywet Hall and Gardens

BUSINESS OFFICE

THE M. O'NEIL CO.

6th Floor

Call on Tuesday Musical Club Tele.—BL-1815

Examination for entrance into the club in October and February. Call the Secretary for information.

Initiation Fee—$5.00. Membership Dues—$5.00.

★ ★ ★

ENTRANCE EXAMINATIONS

REQUIREMENTS

Persons applying for membership in the Club shall meet the following requirements:

Vocal applicants shall have prepared for the Committee an aria from an opera or oratorio, and present four songs.

Piano applicants a Beethoven Sonata, a Chopin Etude and Chopin Nocturne and three pieces from famous composers.

Accompanists shall take the active examination and shall play two songs at sight sung by a member of the Examining Committee.

7

The SEIBERLING SINGERS *dedicate this program in memory of* MRS. F. A. SEIBERLING, *whose untiring lifelong efforts in the field of music and music appreciation were an inspiration to all who knew her.*

THE ROCHESTER PHILHARMONIC ORCHESTRA

Sir Thomas Beecham, Conducting

Thursday, 8:30 p. m. March 28, 1946

Akron Armory

Above: Akron Armory seating chart with ticket prices, 1946

Club members at convention in Columbus, Ohio, in 1951

Reaching Out to a New Generation, 1947–1972

WITH DONATIONS from members like Mary Schumacher and others, Tuesday Musical was able to increase outreach to young musicians, notably through the Brahms Junior Music Club and the Allegro Youth Music Club, both formed in 1949. These youth organizations, as well as individual scholarships for graduating high school seniors, expanded the club's presence and esteem in the community. The organizations and scholarships also ensured that a new generation of music lovers would continue the club's legacy of world-class entertainment and a commitment to the arts. The tireless work of volunteer members also continued, emulating the passion for music and charity of their forebearers.

By 1955, when three hundred people were turned away from a performance of the Ballets Russes at the armory, it became clear that Tuesday Musical needed a new home. Not only was the seating capacity insufficient, the acoustics were poor and the odor of wrestling matches

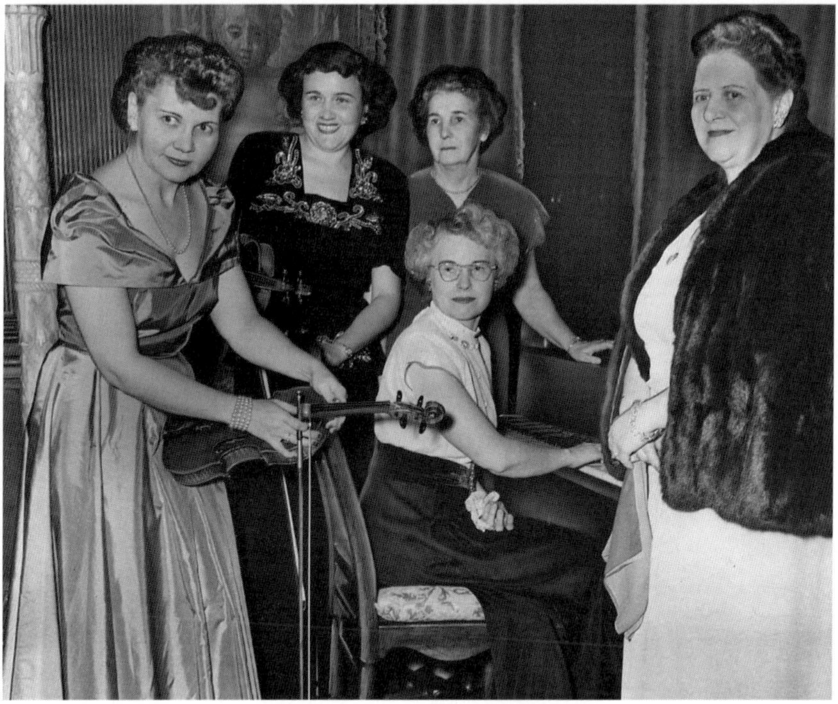

lingered in the air. Mrs. Walter P. Keith, concert chairman at the time, immediately began a campaign for a new auditorium. The search for an appropriate venue was slow and frustrating, but in 1967, when The University of Akron made its transition from a municipal to a state university, the club found hope. Dr. Norman Auburn, the tenth president of the university, had overseen a great expansion after World War II, and he wished to continue the long tradition of close ties between the university and the wider community. Dr. Auburn planned to construct a new performing arts auditorium that could accommodate both civic and scholarly purposes. A tide of support rushed in from businesses, private citizens, and charitable groups, like the Akron Community Foundation, who funded a $50,000 grant for the project. For its part, Tuesday Musical raised $25,000 for the new hall, which they presented to Dr. Auburn in 1968, in honor of Mary Schumacher. Dr. Auburn assured them that the Edwin J. Thomas Performing Arts Hall (named for the former Goodyear CEO who had served on the university's board) would become, upon its completion in 1973, a permanent home

Above: From the *Akron Beacon Journal*, December 11, 1948, Tuesday Musical members perform at Stan Hywet Hall, standing L-R: Marguerite Scheu, Dorothy Merryweather, and Louise Inskeep, seated at the piano, Lora Gillespie, and standing Grace Contraito, photograph by John Neitz for Tuesday Musical. Thus began the warm relationship between the club and the university, which continues to this day.

In Akron, as elsewhere in the nation, the year 1968 was a year of great progress, but also of great social upheaval. That summer, race riots erupted in most cities across the United States, prompted by economic issues and changing cultural attitudes. Akron endured a week of curfews, confrontations between minorities and police, and firebombs lobbed into local businesses. Perhaps prompted by these events, but more likely just weary of the armory's poor facilities, Tuesday Musical made a temporary change of location to the Akron Civic Theatre. Formerly the atmospheric Loew's Theatre, featuring alabaster sculptures and a faux star-lit sky above its auditorium, the theatre was built in 1929 on Main Street, about four blocks away from the armory. Primarily a movie house that also featured live performers, Loew's fell on hard times once television began to rise in popularity. To save the crumbling edifice from being torn down, the Jaycees bought it in 1960, renamed it the Akron Civic Theatre, and transformed it into a locale for civic functions. After almost a decade of struggling financially, the Jaycees launched a campaign to attract better perform-

Above: Congress Lake Country Club Executive and Auxiliary Board Luncheon, May 16, 1950

Oatmeal Legacy Is Music to the Ears

By Ethel Boros

A legacy based on oatmeal and love has enriched Akron area residents.

Mary Schumacher left the legacy to the Tuesday Musical Club of Akron in 1937. She stipulated that it be used for concerts.

It was prompted by her love of music and her money came from an oatmeal fortune accumulated by her husband, Ferdinand Schumacher, founder of the Quaker Oats Co., who died in 1908.

A pianist, Mrs. Schumacher was for many years a faithful member of the 76-year old musical club. The club seeks to "advance the interest of music in the Akron vicinity" and its 175 members are deeply involved in musical projects.

Like other music clubs its members study music and give performances at daytime meetings. They also sponsor professional concerts.

OVER THE YEARS Mrs. Schumacher observed the financial problems encountered by the club in its efforts to bring the finest in music to Akron. When she died she left more than $50,000 to the Tuesday Musical Club to ease the burden of presenting public concerts.

For 13 years the club did nothing to increase its legacy.

But in 1950 the finance committee asked the First National Bank of Akron to re-invest the funds. So competently did bank and committee work together that today the principal is some four times larger than it was originally.

It makes possible an amazingly low-cost, six-concert course presented in Akron Armory. "We look upon it as our contribution to the community," says Mrs. Guido H. Stempel, who is concert chairman.

THE COURSE is available for as little as $5, student price $3. Top price is $14. Prices are kept low to attract as wide an audience as possible.

Each year a portion of the income is used to make up the difference between cost of the concert course and money received from ticket sales.

Akron Armory seats 2,500 and the average attendance is about 2,000, according to Mrs. Stempel. But attendance is rising, she adds.

The Cleveland Orchestra will appear Oct. 15 with George Szell conducting and with Mstislav Rostropovich as cello soloist.

Robert Shaw will conduct the Cleveland Orchestra in its second appearance in March.

ROBERTA PETERS, coloratura soprano of Metropolitan Opera fame, will appear Oct. 29; Lorin Hollander, young American pianist, Nov. 12. The Vienna Choirs Boys will sing Jan. 17 and the Boston Pops Tour Orchestra with Arthur Fiedler as conductor will bring the season to a close April 17.

Organized in 1887, the Tuesday Musical Club is seven years older than its Cleveland counterpart, the Fortnightly Musical Club, and is doubtless the oldest music club in Northern Ohio. The Saint Ceceilia Choral Society was founded in 1921 as an auxiliary society of the club by Mrs. F. A. Seiberling and her daughter, Mrs. Milton Harrison.

In its 76-year history the club has kept its standards high. Most of the world's great artists have appeared in Akron under its auspices. Some child prodigies, such as pianist Josef Hofman and violinist Yehudi Menuhin, later made return engagements as mature artists.

WITH AN ADEQUATE budget the concert committee can consider any sort of concert attraction, including the great European orchestras such as the Vienna Philharmonic. But in the last two years the club has chosen the Cleveland Orchestra because members feel that the American orchestra is among the world's finest, the equal of any European ensemble.

The public concerts are only one of the club's activities. Daytime musicales held in members' homes and guest meetings at the Women's City Club in Akron and in Stan Hywet Hall are well-attended.

Also important are the activities with young people in junior music clubs and the awarding of scholarships for musical study. About $3,000 is dispensed annually for scholarships.

Current president of the group is Mrs. Howser C. Hunt. The Tuesday Musical Club is a member of both the Ohio and the National Federation of Music Clubs.

ers and bigger audiences. Tuesday Musical saw a move to the Civic Theatre in 1971 as an opportunity for both groups to benefit: the club could wait for its new home in the relative luxury of plush seats and Mediterranean decor; the Civic Theatre elevated its reputation with world-class musical performances and enthusiastic audiences.

A new era was dawning for the country, and for the club. The prospect of a new and permanent home for Tuesday Musical refreshed the club's spirit. The music members sought out and shared with their city would play on, whatever the venue, into the future.

MABEL LOUISE LAMBORN GRAHAM, born on July 13, 1905, in Alliance, Ohio, to Lora L. (Loray) and Mabel Teeters Lamborn. Her first name was originally Louise, but in memory of her mother, she took the name Mabel at an early age.

On January 19, 1925, she married Lawrence A. Graham, a dentist, in Wellsburg, West Virginia. By 1927, Dr. Graham's practice was located at 405 East Cuyahoga Falls Avenue and their residence was 417 Cornell, both in Akron. In later years, the practice moved to another building on East Cuyahoga Falls while the Grahams moved to Silver Lake.

During Tuesday Musical's 1932–38 subscription campaigns, Mabel was one of the top, if not the top, ticket sellers. Her tactic was to rise at three or four in the morning and be the first in line at the club's business office, which opened at eight. This ensured her the best choice of tickets for the concerts, so she had the best seats to offer her patrons. Mabel remained active in the club during World War II, holding a six-year term as concert chair (a position now known as concert manager).

In 1949, the *Akron Beacon Journal*'s Business Manager John Barry challenged Mabel to start a local symphony orchestra. Barry provided five hundred dollars in seed money and had two stipulations: the musicians had to be union and Mabel could never give up. Focusing on this challenge, Mabel helped found the Greater Akron Music Association, ultimately the parent organization for the Akron Symphony and its associated choral and youth groups. Prior attempts to create a symphony had failed, in part because financial support was not secured prior to the season. Mabel focused on fund-raising, hosting symphony balls to ensure financial support, before planning upcoming seasons.

In 1977, Mabel became president of Tuesday Musical, part of her twenty-five years of service to the club, which named her a life member in 1995. In 2001, the inaugural year of the Akron Area Arts Alliance's Arts Alive! Awards, Mabel was named Arts Patron for her efforts on behalf of the Akron Symphony and Tuesday Musical.

In addition to being a piano teacher, Mabel spent many years affiliated with the Akron, Cleveland, Northfield, and Lake Placid skating clubs, serving as an international figure skating judge until her retirement at age seventy-five. She died in Stow on August 2, 2002.

Opposite: From the *Cleveland Plain Dealer*, September 22, 1963

LOLA MAE SECOR ROTHMANN was born May 6, 1923, in Jamestown, Pennsylvania, the daughter of Percy A. and Carolyn Owen Secor. While her father supported his family by working for the Postal Service, he was a known local pianist and a graduate of the Conservatory of Music in Warren, Pennsylvania.

Lola was a 1941 graduate of Jamestown High. She married Dr. Bruce F. Rothmann of Cuyahoga Falls on June 14, 1947, a year before his graduation from New York University's College of Medicine. By 1954, after Bruce's graduate work at the University of Pennsylvania, they settled in Cuyahoga Falls and Bruce began his practice in Akron, specializing in pediatric surgery.

In 1970, Lola was asked to temporarily cover the Tuesday Musical concert manager duties while the incumbent, Pat Hunt, traveled abroad with her husband. During this trial-by-fire, the ensemble scheduled for the opening concert of the season cancelled one week before the performance. As Lola's temporary duties extended into a year, there were several other cancellations and weather challenges. Nevertheless, Lola volunteered for the job for the following nineteen years. Each year she faced the challenges of artist contract negotiations, marketing, program production, and budgeting, as well as hosting post-concert receptions and providing transportation services for artists.

In 1984, building on the knowledge Lola gained as Tuesday Musical's concert manager, and their mutual love of music, Lola and Bruce became cofounders of the Music at Stan Hywet Hall concerts. This series later evolved into Music from the Western Reserve.

In 1989, when Lola stepped down as concert manager, Tuesday Musical honored her with the creation of the Lola Rothmann Volunteer Achievement Award. Lola continued as concert manager for Music from the Western Reserve until 2004.

In November 2005, the Akron Area Arts Alliance awarded both Lola and Bruce the Lifetime Achievement Award for their support of the arts. While Bruce died in 2006 after fifty-nine years of marriage, Lola continues her support of the arts today.

Program from the November 30, 1948 Clifford Curzon concert

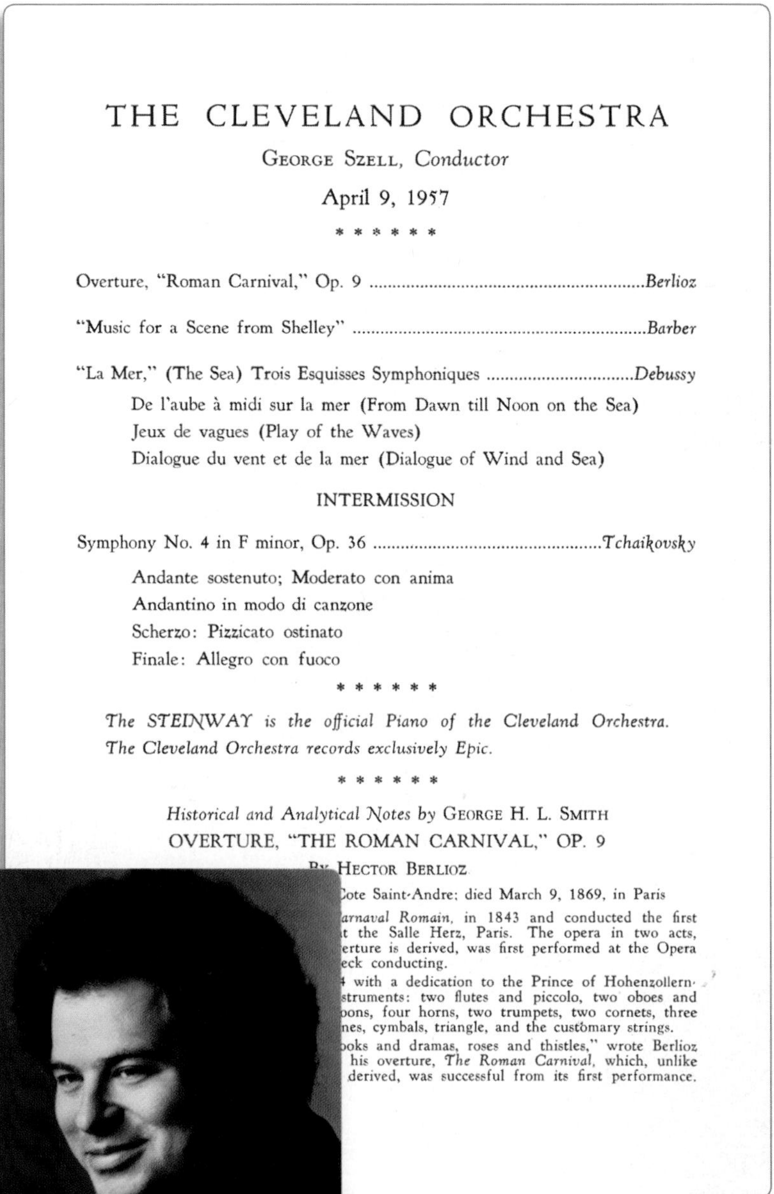

THE CLEVELAND ORCHESTRA

GEORGE SZELL, *Conductor*

April 9, 1957

* * * * * *

Overture, "Roman Carnival," Op. 9 .... *Berlioz*

"Music for a Scene from Shelley" .... *Barber*

"La Mer," (The Sea) Trois Esquisses Symphoniques .... *Debussy*

De l'aube à midi sur la mer (From Dawn till Noon on the Sea)
Jeux de vagues (Play of the Waves)
Dialogue du vent et de la mer (Dialogue of Wind and Sea)

INTERMISSION

Symphony No. 4 in F minor, Op. 36 .... *Tchaikovsky*

Andante sostenuto; Moderato con anima
Andantino in modo di canzone
Scherzo: Pizzicato ostinato
Finale: Allegro con fuoco

* * * * * *

The STEINWAY is the official Piano of the Cleveland Orchestra.
The Cleveland Orchestra records exclusively Epic.

* * * * * *

Historical and Analytical Notes by GEORGE H. L. SMITH

OVERTURE, "THE ROMAN CARNIVAL," OP. 9

By HECTOR BERLIOZ

...ote Saint-Andre; died March 9, 1869, in Paris

...*arnaval Romain*, in 1843 and conducted the first ...t the Salle Herz, Paris. The opera in two acts, ...erture is derived, was first performed at the Opera ...eck conducting.

...4 with a dedication to the Prince of Hohenzollern-...struments: two flutes and piccolo, two oboes and ...oons, four horns, two trumpets, two cornets, three ...nes, cymbals, triangle, and the customary strings.

...ooks and dramas, roses and thistles," wrote Berlioz ... his overture, *The Roman Carnival*, which, unlike ... derived, was successful from its first performance.

Above, clockwise from top: Program from the April 9, 1957 Cleveland Orchestra concert; Publicity photo of Itzhak Perlman

Opposite: Poster advertising Jascha Heifetz's February 21, 1950 concert

Heifetz
AKRON ARMORY
FEB. 21, 1950 - 8:30 p.m.
presented by The Tuesday Musical Club
Box Office - 6th Floor - The M. O'Neil Co. - BI 1815

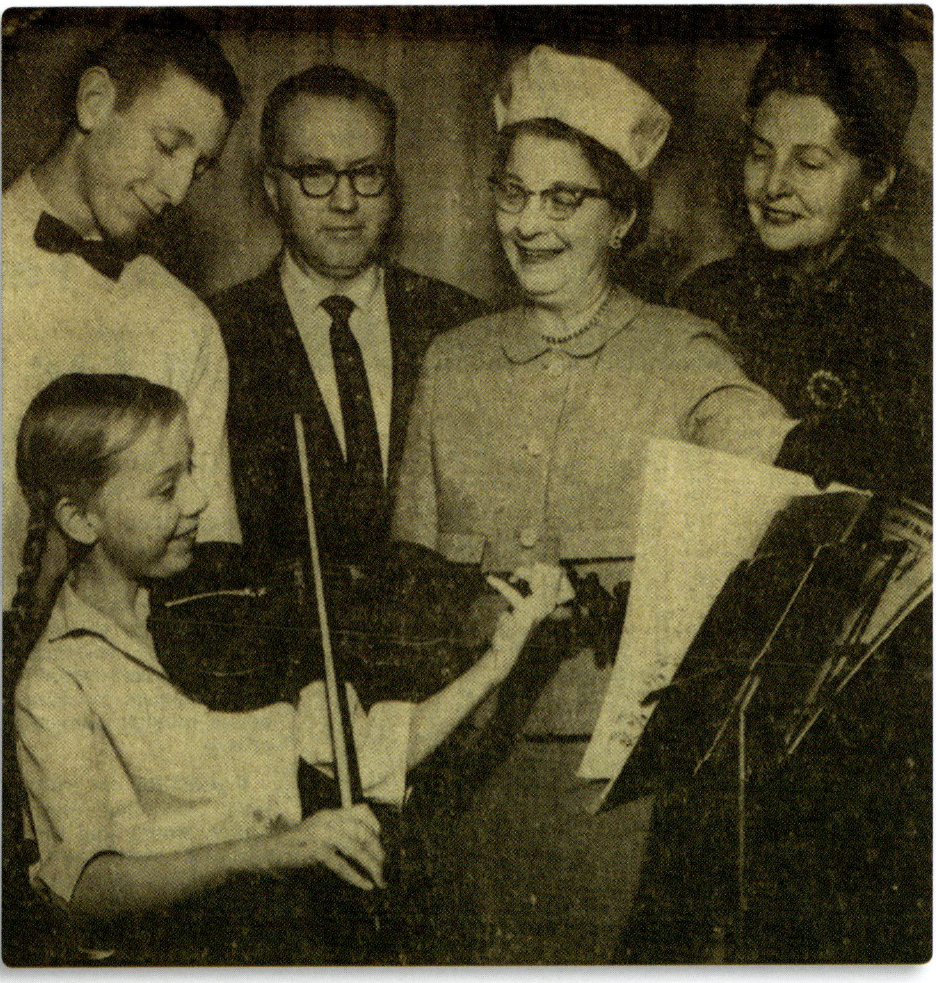

Clockwise from top: From the *Akron Beacon Journal*, January 13, 1966, Mrs. Richard Irvin (left),and Mrs. Milton Nelson (right) members of Tuesday Musical, participated in the club's program at Stan Hywet

Opposite, clockwise from top: From the *Akron Beacon Journal,* May 3, 1964, Jane Meyer plays for (from left), Dan Buie, a junior in music at UA, her teacher; Dr. Farley K. Hutchins, head of the UA music department; Mrs. Howser Hunt, president of the Tuesday Musical, and Mrs. Hugh Colopy, chairman of the club's scholarship committee; Tuesday Musical gathering, Portage Country Club, Akron, Ohio, May 17, 1966

Above: From the *Akron Beacon Journal,* June 28, 1968, Tuesday Musical scholarship winners (front, from left) Lynn Schumber, Charles Olegar, (back, from left) Peter Bambakidis, William Nesbitt, and James Grosjean

Opposite, clockwise from top: Letter to Mrs. Guido Stempel regarding the Schumacher bequest; From the *Akron Beacon Journal,* January 9, 1966

LAW OFFICES
BUCKINGHAM, DOOLITTLE & BURROUGHS
SECOND NATIONAL BUILDING
AKRON, OHIO 44308

TELEPHONE 535-2661
AREA CODE 216

LISLE M. BUCKINGHAM
GILLUM H. DOOLITTLE
EDMUND BURROUGHS
CHARLES F. SCANLON
HERMAN E. RABE
HUGH COLOPY
DWIGHT PARSONS
WILLIAM T. WALKER
RICHARD A. CHENOWETH
ALLAN JOHNSON
L. ANDREW REED, JR.
DUANE MORRIS

CHARLES E. PIERSON
KENNETH G. HUMER
JOHN M. GLENN
EDWARD C. KAMINSKI
JAMES S. PEDLER, JR.
TIMOTHY F. SCANLON
FREDERICK M. LOMBARDI
DENNIS L. TRAVIS
DONALD A. POWELL
DANIEL G. LAPORTE
DENNIS SHAUL

February 29, 1968

Mrs. Guido H. Stempel
3022 Oakridge Drive
Silver Lake
Cuyahoga Falls, Ohio 44224

Re: Will of Mary Z. Schumacher

Dear Mrs. Stempel:

At your request, I obtained from the courthouse and am enclosing herewith a certified copy of the Last Will and Testament of Mary Z. Schumacher. The provision which is particularly applicable to the Tuesday Musical Club is Item XI, which reads as follows:

> "After all these bequests have been made, I bequeath the rest of my estate--one-half to the Sumner Home for the Aged and the other half to the Tuesday Musical Club for concerts. If there is no Tuesday Musical Club, the money is to be given to the Y. W. C. A. in memory of my husband, Mr. Ferdinand Schumacher."

You have asked for our opinion as to whether a bequest from the principal of such fund to the Center for Performing Arts would be authorized under the terms of the will of Mary Z. Schumacher. For the reasons stated hereafter, it would be our opinion that such a bequest would be within both the spirit and the letter of Mrs. Schumacher's will.

The will creates no trust, but rather makes an outright bequest to the Tuesday Musical Club and it is my understanding that the funds have been held in an agency agreement with First National Bank of Akron.

Participate In Club Musicale

EARL KELLY will play a piano solo to open the program for Tuesday Musical Club at 1:30 p. m. Tuesday in Stan Hywet Carriage House. He is a member of the Kent State University faculty in the Conservatory of Music.

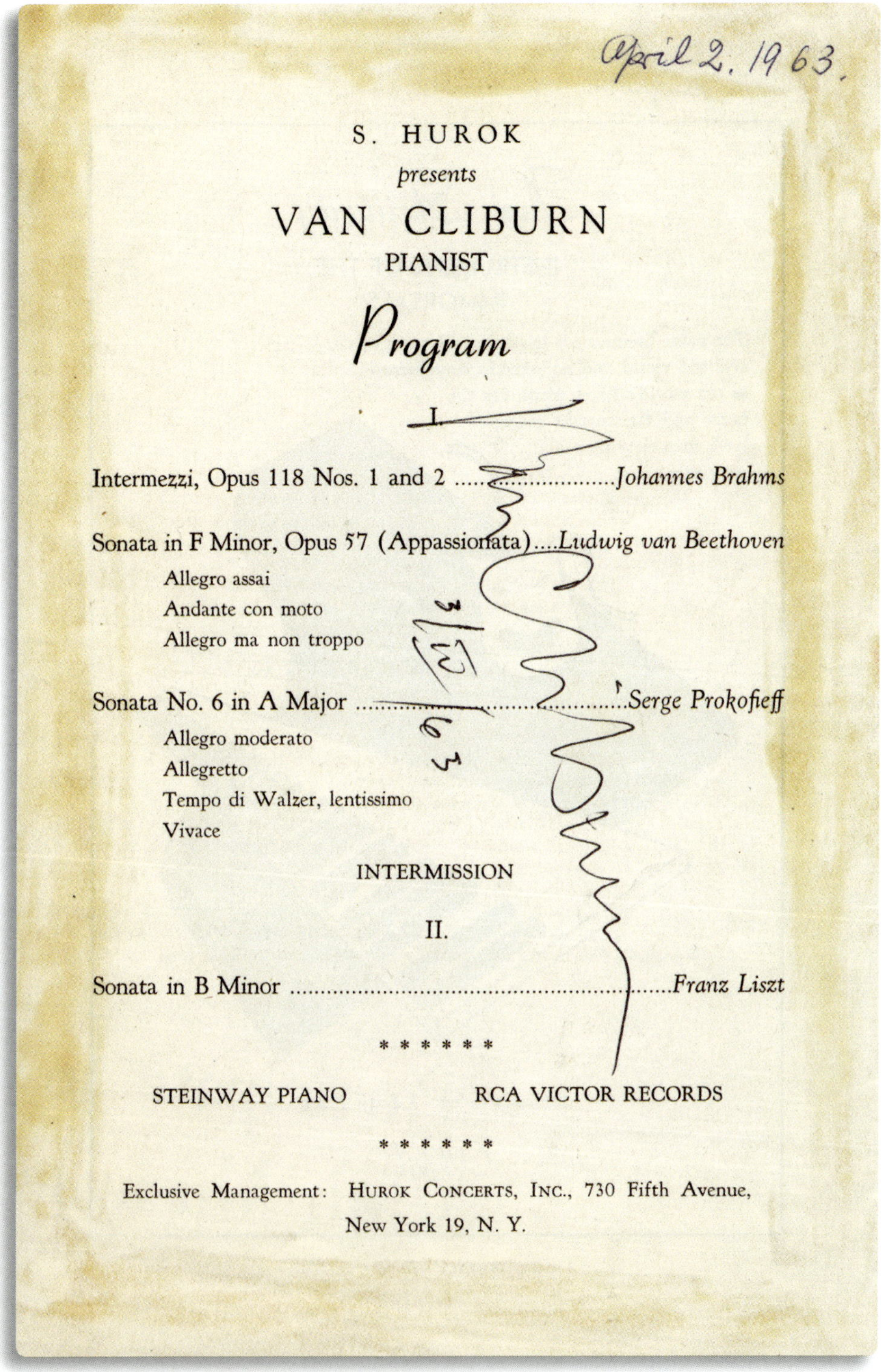

April 2, 1963.

S. HUROK

presents

VAN CLIBURN

PIANIST

Program

I.

Intermezzi, Opus 118 Nos. 1 and 2 .... *Johannes Brahms*

Sonata in F Minor, Opus 57 (Appassionata) .... *Ludwig van Beethoven*

- Allegro assai
- Andante con moto
- Allegro ma non troppo

Sonata No. 6 in A Major .... *Serge Prokofieff*

- Allegro moderato
- Allegretto
- Tempo di Walzer, lentissimo
- Vivace

INTERMISSION

II.

Sonata in B Minor .... *Franz Liszt*

* * * * * *

STEINWAY PIANO RCA VICTOR RECORDS

* * * * * *

Exclusive Management: HUROK CONCERTS, INC., 730 Fifth Avenue, New York 19, N. Y.

From the Van Cliburn program, with artist's autograph, March 1963

Play On, into the Future, 1973–Present

IN 1973, upon completion of the Edwin J. Thomas Performing Arts Hall, Tuesday Musical settled into their new home at The University of Akron. The hall provided a comfortable and accommodating locale for Tuesday Musical to continue its tradition of bringing the most sought-after artists to Akron. Luciano Pavarotti, Joan Sutherland, and Beverly Sills, among others, entertained large audiences in the hall's acoustically impressive and architecturally stunning theater. In 1987, the club celebrated its centennial anniversary with performances by Itzhak Perlman, Empire Brass, the King's Singers, and, of course, the Cleveland Orchestra. The latter found a new summer home for itself in Cuyahoga Falls, at the outdoor Blossom Music Center, but its long relationship with Tuesday Musical continued as warmly as ever.

In 1995, then concert manager Barbara Feld began nudging the club into increasingly experimental musical territory with concerts by avant-guard groups like the Kronos Quartet and eighth blackbird.

Members of St. Cecelia Chorus, Christmas 2007

Feld also helped strengthen Tuesday Musical's relationship with The University of Akron's School of Music by cosponsoring operatic productions that involved both student and professional guest performers. In keeping with the group's reorganization as Tuesday Musical Association in 2005, a new position was created for Feld—that of executive director. Feld continued to steer the group into the future, always looking for ways to spark interest in the younger generation.

In 2008, Feld began the *FUZE!* concert series—in conjunction with the Akron Art Museum—for exactly that reason. The series presented concerts in the art museum's intimate 160-seat Charles and Jane Lehner Auditorium, featuring classically-trained artists who stretched the traditional boundaries of classical music. Performers like the string quartet ETHEL and the electric violinist Tracy Silverman tested new musical frontiers and helped Akronites broaden their musical sensibilities. A key component of this series was creating a connection between the artists and local students, from elementary school through the university level. The artists engaged students in workshops and lecture/demonstrations whenever there was a FUZE! performance. This

Tuesday Musical Annual Meeting, 2008

dynamic of education through performance continued the original purpose of Tuesday Musical, linking the past to the future.

Tuesday Musical's spirit of charity and community involvement continues in the twenty-first century. In the summer of 2012, an anonymous donation of a hundred thousand dollars made it possible for Tuesday Musical to acquire a new Steinway Concert Grand Model D piano. The University of Akron helped facilitate the acquisition by trading in one of its twenty-five-year-old concert grands toward the purchase. Feld notes that the new instrument was long overdue, as performers were complaining about the treble range on the older pianos. The sleek, nine-foot grand with an ebonized finish was named "The Three Graces" in honor of three women who encouraged the donor to make music a vital part of his or her life. Grammy-winning American pianist Emanuel Ax was first to test the ivories on the E. J. Thomas Hall stage. His grand chords reverberated through the hall, much as Tuesday Musical's ongoing legacy of fine music and community engagement continues to resonate with music lovers in Akron.

Emanuel Ax gets the feel of the new Steinway prior to his September 2012 concert

MARGARET CATHERINE BARTHEL BAXTRESSER, the daughter of William Thade Barthel and Jennet Mable MacLean, was born June 10, 1922, in Detroit, Michigan. Her early aptitude for music led to her debut with the Detroit Orchestra at age thirteen. In 1941 she met Earl Walz Baxtresser, an avid amateur pianist; they were married in 1942. Margaret continued her concert career, winning the prestigious Walter W. Naumburg Foundation piano competition in 1950.

The Baxtressers spent their early years in the Philadelphia and Minneapolis areas; Margaret continued to perform with major orchestras in the United States and Europe. In 1966, Earl's position with Goodyear led the family to Akron. Margaret maintained a professional career and served on the piano faculty of Kent State University from 1966 through 1991, while raising their four children and two foster daughters.

Margaret's musical involvement included decades of association with Tuesday Musical, as well as the Cuyahoga Valley Arts Ensemble, the Children's Concert Society, and, later, the Seneca Trio. She encouraged multiple music organizations by hosting recitals and receptions in the South Rose Avenue home she shared with Earl. Her involvement did not wane after his death on June 3, 1991.

On February 20, 1994, Margaret became the first American to perform in Vietnam since 1964. Her performance was a goodwill gesture, spurred by contact with visiting ethno-musicologist Dr. Phong Nguyen and his wife, Tuyen Tonnu. In 1995, Margaret returned as the featured soloist with the Vietnam National Symphony Orchestra, marking the fiftieth anniversary of the United Nations. In October 2004, she donated her music collection to the Hanoi Conservatory.

In recognition for Margaret's many efforts to support the music community, she received the 2001 Outstanding Artist Award for Music at the Akron Area Arts Alliance's first Arts Alive! Awards. She actively attended performances and supported the music scene until her death from a stroke on June 8, 2005. Since 2007, in recognition of her many contributions, Tuesday Musical has presented an annual Margaret Baxtresser Piano Concert.

BARBARA FELD, the daughter of Harold and Irene Reid, was born on July 5, 1943, in St. Louis, Missouri. She attended the University of Missouri in St. Louis, majoring in English. After her marriage to aeronautical engineer Denis J. Feld, also from St. Louis, the couple relocated to Akron, Ohio, in 1978. Upon arriving in Akron, Barbara worked for a short time as an engineer's aide at Goodyear Aerospace Corporation, joining Tuesday Musical in 1982.

From 1984 until 1989, Barbara acted as Tuesday Musical's advertising coordinator; upon the retirement of Lola Rothmann in 1989, she became concert manager. In 1995, Barbara broadened the scope of Tuesday Musical concerts with the trend-setting engagement of the Kronos Quartet. In recognition of the efforts of Barbara, Lola Rothmann, and Mabel Graham to promote classical music and Tuesday Musical in Northeast Ohio, the three were co-winners of the 1995–96 *Northern Ohio Live* classical music achievement award.

During the 2006 season, Barbara introduced the Margaret Baxtresser Annual Piano Concert, named after one of Tuesday Musical's greatest advocates. Barbara's work for Tuesday Musical began as a part-time position and quickly segued into a full-time plus position. Her unofficial title was 'Artistic Director,' as she worked arduously with Tuesday Musical members and community leaders to select artists for each season. Her initial passion was to bring the best artists to Akron, but over the years that became intrinsically married to her vision for education and community outreach. Barbara, along with other Tuesday Musical volunteers, expanded the ticket voucher program for students and seniors; she also supported the commission and debut of new works.

Collaboration has been Barbara's strong point, starting with *FUZE*'s 2008 debut. This joint venture with the Akron Art Museum introduced contemporary ensembles to a new, younger audience, receiving the 2009 Akron Area Arts Alliance's Arts Alive Collaborative Project Award. Subsequent collaborative educational outreach projects have included PNC Bank's Grow Up Great program, the Ohio Arts Council IMPACT Tour, and Summa Health's Healing Arts Program, among others. Tuesday Musical's participation was recognized by the 2011 Akron Area Arts Alliance Outreach Award, while Barbara received the 2011 Margaret Clark Morgan Foundation Impact Award.

Eva Mae Yockey

One of the most fascinating characters I've ever written about is a woman I never met. In the fall of 1998, a brief item ran in the *Akron Beacon Journal*, reporting that Tuesday Musical had received an enigmatic donation of more than half a million dollars—one of the largest individual gifts ever to any Akron cultural organization, and more than ten times larger than Tuesday Musical had ever seen.

But nobody had ever heard of the donor, Eva Mae Yockey. Nobody knew her motivation for the gift. And nobody knew where to begin unraveling her mystery. I went looking.

Her story unfolded like layers of an onion, interview by interview, emerging from small-town public records and fragmented memories from neighbors and family.

Above: Arden and Eva Mae Yockey, from the *Akron Beacon Journal*, October 24, 1968

Eva Mae Yockey was a reclusive schoolteacher from rural Dover Township who worked thirty-three years in the Kent City Schools, socializing very little outside the school building, renting a room in town and returning each weekend to the family farmhouse on Columbia Road, a home she lived in her whole life. To most neighbors in the small Ohio town, she was a modest loner, an eccentric whose lights stayed on all night and who never came out during the day. But Eva Yockey had a secret, one she'd held since a troubled childhood: Before she died, she wanted to make a million dollars.

When she retired in 1973, she invested a savings of $2,500. Through careful tending, market research, some additional inheritance money and canny investing, she managed to achieve her life goal. Even as her home deteriorated and neighbors whispered about her sanity, she quietly and resolutely built her fortune. Her estate was worth $1,067,936.50.

And when she died, she gave it all away. A quarter of it to a neighbor, a quarter to a Carroll County residential facility for adults with mental retardation. And half to Tuesday Musical, in honor of her brother Arden Yockey, a Norton music teacher who regularly took his students to Tuesday Musical performances.

And so the Yockey name emerged from a shroud of intrigue to the memorial name on a wide series of scholarships, a strange legacy that will forever be part of the Tuesday Musical story.

—David Giffels

BEVERLY
SILLS
COLORATURA SOPRANO
NEW YORK CITY OPERA
ROYAL OPERA HOUSE COVENT GARDEN, LONDON
TEATRO ALLA SCALA, MILAN
TEATRO COLON, BUENOS AIRES
TEATRO SAN CARLO, NAPLES
TUESDAY MUSICAL CONCERTS
WEDNESDAY, JAN. 24, 1973
8:15 P.M.
AKRON CIVIC THEATRE
182 S. MAIN ST. ● AKRON, OHIO
Tickets $5, $4, $3, Students $1
Phone 762-3115
Mon. thru Fri.
9 a.m. to 4 p.m.

E2 Akron Beacon Journal Wednesday, May 9, 1979

Musical birthday for choral group

Polly Paffilas
About town

It was a musical gathering when St. Cecelia Choral Society marked the beginning of its 59th year. The guest day program and luncheon was held at the home of **Francis Albrecht.**

The hostess was a few minutes late because she had another meeting that morning. However, **Ruth Elaine Steere,** co-hostess, did a fine job of meeting and greeting folks.

Elaine Ashcroft, society president, started off the program with several numbers, including the aria from "Mignon." Elaine, a mezzo-soprano, sings with the Cleveland Chorus, and has appeared with the San Francisco and Dallas operas.

Elaine's voice really soared. She was accompanied by **Donna Geller,** a member of Tuesday Musical Club.

More beautiful songs were presented by the chorus, directed by **Elizabeth Crater,** a Barberton resident. Soloist was **Mary Lou Childress.** The piano accompaniment was provided by **Isabel Infield,** whose daughter, **Ruth Hunt,** sings in the chorus.

This was the second performance of the day for Mrs. Infield and Ruth. Earlier that morning, they were on the program for the Women's Fellowship at Silver Lake Congregational Church.

THE CHORAL SOCIETY, an offshoot of Tuesday Musical Club, was organized in the spring of 1921. **Mrs. F. A. Seiberling** and her daughter, **Irene Harrison Seiberling,**

Beacon Journal photo by Paul Tople

Mezzo-soprano Elaine Ashcroft
...with accompanist Donna Geller

suggested to **Mrs. H. S. Bowman,** then Tuesday Club president, that a choral society be formed for daughters and daughters-in-law of Tuesday Club members, who were musically inclined.

The first meeting was held at the home of **Mrs. George Stadelman,** "Grey Lodge," which is now the Akron Woman's City Club.

During the early years, the society put on annual musical programs at Mrs. Seiberling's home, Stan Hywet, in the music room, which Mrs. Seiberling had especially built for Tuesday Club.

Besides singing for themselves, the members of St. Cecelia Society (named for the patron saint of music), present programs at Rockynol, Sumner Home and church groups in the area.

CHARTER MEMBERS still active are Mrs. Harrison, **Grace Williams, Ethylene Foltz, Ruth Oenslager and Harriet Parke.**

Other officers serving with Elaine Ashcroft are **Ruth Lucas,** vice president; **Peggy Elias,** secretary, and **Gloria Hepburn,** treasurer.

Over the luncheon of chicken salad and marinated vegetables, **Peg Brewster** told about the Stan Hywet tour to historic Charleston, S.C.

Nina Gottwald just came home from California, where she attended the wedding of her grandson, **Peter Schuyler Gottwald,** in Walnut Creek.

Music and art

There will be listening and dancing music at the Akron Art Institute Saturday from 7 p.m. to 10 p.m. at the free, open-to-the-public party to introduce the five new exhibits.

On view through June 24 will be Willem de Kooning paintings and sculpture, Donald Judd sculpture and photographs by Diane Arbus, Mark Cohen and by Brassai, the name adopted by Gyula Halasz, who was born in Transylvania and who took the name of the town of his birth.

Another event this week at the Art Institute is a seminar on contemporary sculpture conducted by **Robert Morris.** It will be Friday from 2:30 to 5 p.m., and is open to all. A reception for the artist will be held from 5 to 7 p.m.

Morris' visit is the first in a series of artist-in-residence programs at the institute made possible by a grant from the National Endowment for the Arts, a federal agency.

Morris is designing a work of sculpture for the rear of Akron Federal Building on Main Street.

The institute is at 69 E. Market St. Admission and parking are free.

Opposite: Handbill advertising Beverly Sills' 1973 concert
Above: From the *Akron Beacon Journal*, May 9, 1979

THE TUESDAY MUSICAL CLUB

Centennial
Anniversary Season
1887-1987

TUESDAY MUSICAL CLUB
E. J. Thomas Performing Arts Hall
Center and Hill Streets
Akron, Ohio 44325
762-3115

Free detailed brochure upon request

100th SEASON 1987 – 1988 CONCERT SERIES
EDWIN J. THOMAS PERFORMING ARTS HALL

Tuesday, October 6, 1987	EMPIRE BRASS
Tuesday, November 24, 1987	THE KING'S SINGERS
Wednesday, December 2, 1987	RUDOLF SERKIN, pianist
Tuesday, February 9, 1988	NEW YORK CITY OPERA NATIONAL COMPANY Beverly Sills, General Director *BARBER OF SEVILLE*
Tuesday, March 29, 1988	CLEVELAND INSTITUTE OF MUSIC SYMPHONY ORCHESTRA LOUIS LANE conducting NAVAH PERLMAN, pianist
Sunday, May 15, 1988	THE CLEVELAND ORCHESTRA CHRISTOPH VON DOHNÁNYI conducting

CENTENNIAL SPECIAL
Non-Subscription Concert
Tuesday, May 10, 1988
ITZHAK PERLMAN, violinist

Opposite, clockwise from top: Audience for the Five Browns, photograph by Margaret Hunter; Advertisement for the 100th anniversary season, 1987–88;

Above: Advertisement for Verdi's *La Traviata*, coproduced by Tuesday Musical and The University of Akron School of Music, 1990, from the *Akron Beacon Journal*, February 18, 1990

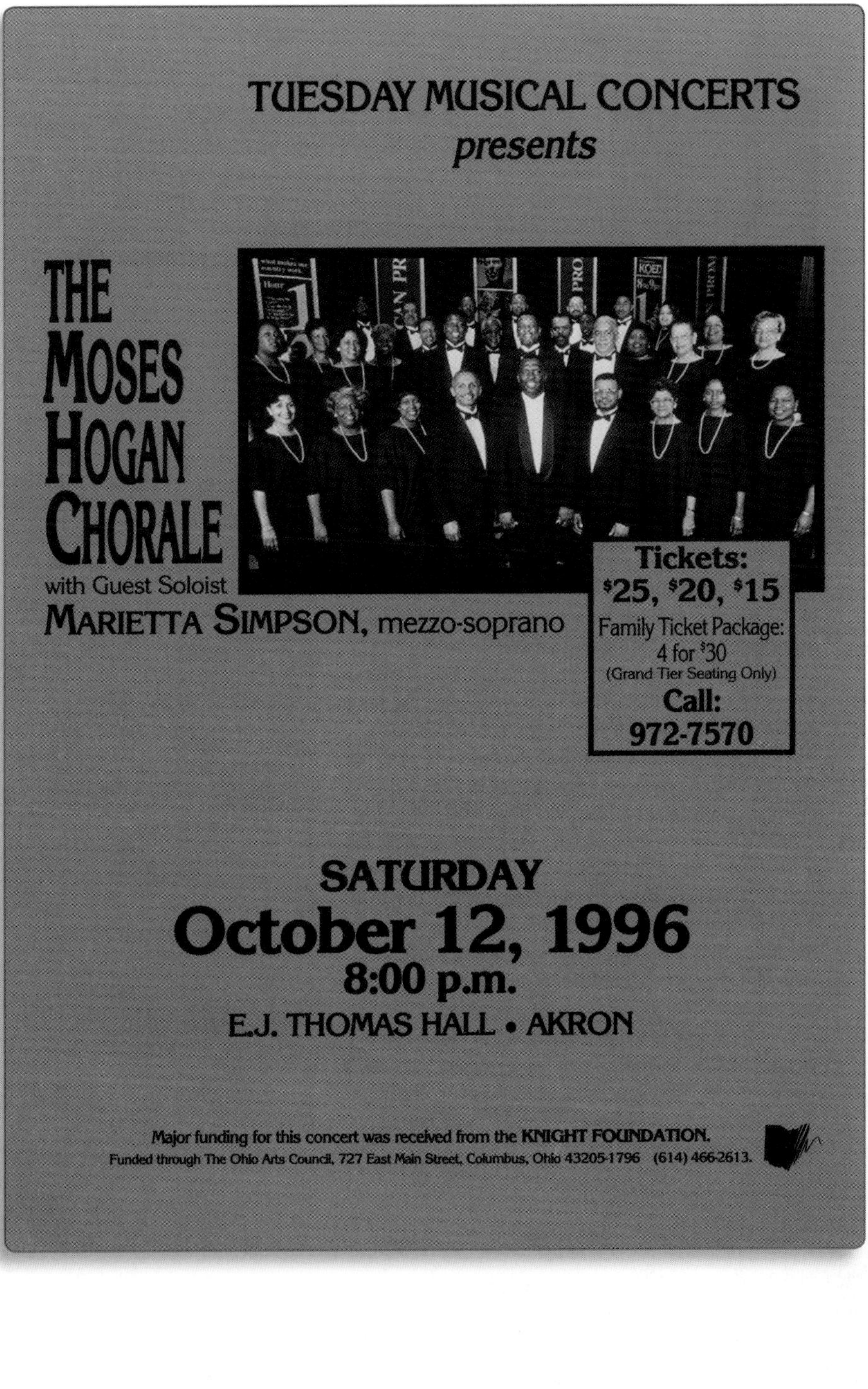
TUESDAY MUSICAL CONCERTS
presents
THE MOSES HOGAN CHORALE
with Guest Soloist
MARIETTA SIMPSON, mezzo-soprano
Tickets:
$25, $20, $15
Family Ticket Package:
4 for $30
(Grand Tier Seating Only)
Call:
972-7570
SATURDAY
October 12, 1996
8:00 p.m.
E.J. THOMAS HALL • AKRON
Major funding for this concert was received from the KNIGHT FOUNDATION.
Funded through The Ohio Arts Council, 727 East Main Street, Columbus, Ohio 43205-1796 (614) 466-2613.

COMMENTARY

Mourning a nurturing friend in music ed

Margaret Baxtresser leaves mark in Akron

By Elaine Guregian
Beacon Journal music writer

Pianist Margaret Baxtresser with one of her three pianos last year. The Bechstein piano was built in Berlin in 1878.

PHIL MASTURZO/Akron Beacon Journal file photo

Akron without pianist Margaret Baxtresser just doesn't seem possible. With her death Tuesday following a stroke, we have lost a vital and supremely nurturing force.

Margaret was one of the wisest and kindest people I have ever known. I will miss her terribly.

It is rare to come across someone as innately thoughtful as Margaret. When I moved to Akron, I was assigned almost immediately to travel to Hong Kong and Japan on tour with the Cleveland Orchestra. I didn't know a soul in the group. Margaret contacted a couple of her friends in the orchestra, one of them the concertmaster, and asked them to say hello. There was nothing in it for her, but a lot for me, which to me is the definition of graciousness.

In the 15 years I knew Margaret, she was always at the hub of Akron's classical music community. Countless times when I was working on a story, it turned out that she was a part of it, or could steer me to someone who was.

I admired her determination. No matter what setbacks there were, nationally or locally, she continued to speak out for the arts. Looking back through the Beacon Journal archives, I came across an article she had written in 1973. In it, she spelled out the many reasons Akronites should take pride in the wealth of musical offerings here. At the end, she noted that the one thing Akron really needed was a music school or conservatory to offer pre-college training. She took the opportunity to suggest what such a conservatory could offer, and where it might be housed.

But then, she always had ideas about how Akron could improve itself. Often, she went back to the need for music education. For the last several years, she volunteered her services to the Children's Concert Society. Always savvy, she knew that small children wouldn't want to sit still for a regular recital. She told me that before she went to schools to play, she thought hard about how to keep the attention of her young audience.

Judy DeShon, a spokeswoman for Children's Concert Society, told me that during an interview on a public access television program in 2003, Margaret said of her Children's Concert Society performances, "I have played literally all over the world. I feel that what I'm doing here for these children is the most significant thing I have done in my life."

Margaret was proud of the success of a program at Tuesday Musical that gave students a way to hear world-renowned musicians free. And Margaret opened her home to children in the Brahms Allegro Club, showing them the fine points of concert etiquette: how to bow, how to shake hands, and so on. This veteran knew that being a musician consisted of much more than sitting at a keyboard and rattling off notes. She had a gift for seeing the big picture and helping others to see it, too.

Another mark of Margaret's graciousness was the way she could go with the flow. Shortly before she died, my daughter and I were at her house for a reception. Zoe, age 9, mentioned that she would like to play the piano. Without another thought, Margaret asked her which one (she owned three) Zoe would prefer. No matter that the house was full of people. Margaret had time to show a little girl up to the music room. There, Zoe had the thrill of playing the historic Bechstein piano that Brahms and Mahler also had played.

Margaret, who would have turned 83 today, spoke often, and fondly, of her own children and grandchildren. Her daughter, Jeanne, who became a professional flutist and teacher, once told me how grateful she was that her mother had allowed her to try a number of instruments before she found the one that suited her.

Interviewed 30 years ago about her teaching methods, Margaret told the Beacon Journal that a teacher's positive attitude was essential. "The lesson shouldn't be a report card, but an opening of doors. I try to encourage them in everything they attempt. And I try to choose repertory which doesn't defeat or demean them at the level they have reached," she said.

Her way was always to encourage, to find the good and make it better. If that sounds old-fashioned, it is, in the best sense of the word.

Another refreshing virtue was Margaret's discretion and tact. She always knew more than she told. Besides losing a community leader, her many friends are also losing a trusted confidante and sounding board.

Margaret sometimes arrived at concerts a little out of breath, having just rushed there from another event. And still, if you were talking to her, you had her complete attention. It was inspiring to see how much she squeezed into every day, not just for herself but for others. We are better for having had her in our lives.

Elaine Guregian is the classical music writer for the Akron Beacon Journal. She can be reached at eguregian@thebeaconjournal.com or 330-996-3574.

Above, clockwise from top: From the *Akron Beacon Journal,* June 10, 2005; A young student plays the harp at an afternoon recital

Opposite: Handbill advertising the Moses Hogan Chorale's 1996 concert

Singer's lesson pitch perfect

Students' voices come alive at master class under the direction of mezzo-soprano

By Elaine Guregian
Beacon Journal music writer

Whether you're singing the role of a maid or a countess, you need to show the audience what makes you tick.

That was the recurring message that mezzo-soprano Frederica von Stade gave at a University of Akron opera master class on Monday. It was a prelude to her appearance tonight in recital with Samuel Ramey, bass, on the Tuesday Musical series at E.J. Thomas Hall.

During her long career performing at the Metropolitan Opera and around the world, von Stade, 60, said she had learned how important it is to let listeners understand the subtext – why your character does what she does.

A beautiful voice is thrilling, she said. But what audiences enjoy most is the intention and the ideas the singer is putting across, she said, noting "even the most perfect (voices) aren't perfect."

Dressed in slacks paired with a shirt and sweater, von Stade looked casually elegant but acted decidedly undivaesque on Tuesday. Perched on the edge of her

LEW STAMP/Akron Beacon Journal photos

Frederica von Stade, (left) a renowned mezzo-soprano, offers performance suggestions to student Jennifer Norman during a master class at University of Akron's Guzzetta Hall on Monday.

supportive ways.

Romanina Campea, Jennifer Norman, Amanda Hermann, Metra Wright, Julie Craigo and Jung Eun Oh represented the University of Akron, Cleveland State University, Kent State University and Baldwin-Wallace College at the master class.

Von Stade complimented the singers as well as their accompanists, coaches and teachers. "Whatever is going on here is marvelous," she said.

Nerves are always an issue, especially when you're young, von Stade said, but they're not

University of Akron student Jennifer Norman sings Gabriel Faure's *Notre Amour* during a master class on Monday.

Details

Concert: Frederica von Stade, mezzo-soprano, and Samuel Ramey, bass
Where: E.J. Thomas Hall, 198 Hill St., Akron
When: 8 tonight
Cost: $40 and $50
Information: 330-972-7570

well-known pieces from that opera.

To Amanda Hermann, a soprano who sang *Porgi amor*, von Stade urged thinking about the big picture of *The Marriage of Figaro* and holding back during this pensive aria. Hermann has a big voice that projects well. "It would be absolutely thrilling if you made us want to hear all of your voice" by holding back here and only singing full-out later, von Stade said.

Von Stade helped Jennifer Norman choose which words to emphasize so audiences would understand the thrust of Gabriel Faure's quickly flowing song *Notre Amour* (Our Love). After Norman tried it again, von Stade congratulated her, "Wonderful! I'm getting your thoughts."

Plotting and planning aren't things that only devious opera characters do.

During this two-hour session, one of the world's most recognized opera stars taught these young singers

---

November 29, 2007

RECEIVED
DEC 0 3 2007

Dear Members of the Tuesday Musical Association,

Hearing a world-renowned musician is usually a once-in-a-lifetime opportunity. Thanks to the Tuesday Musical Association, my students and I get the chance to hear some of the finest musicians in the world each and every year! Offering students free tickets and a free bus ride to the concert is often the only way to get them to a concert of this caliber. The wonderful thing is that once I take them they are hooked forever. The students love the concert experience and are always buzzing about the performance the whole ride home. Yo-Yo Ma has been a featured performer for Tuesday Musical Association two times, and each and every time the students attending the concert were astounded by his musicianship and also by his approachable personality. The Cleveland Orchestra is also a concert that all of us look forward to. Thanks to you and to your sponsors for giving my students this opportunity. It is often the catalyst that encourages them to become patrons of the arts as adults. Thank you for your work to organize this outstanding program and please know that it is important to our future.

Sincerely,

Michele N. Monigold
Jackson Instrumental Music Department

Instruments to be collected tonight for needy students

WAPS radio will have table at Tuesday Musical program at E.J. Thomas Hall

Tuesday Musical has partnered with WAPS (91.3-FM) to provide musical instruments to students who can't afford them.

At tonight's piano recital by Garrick Ohlsson, Tommy Bruno of WAPS will accept instrument donations. Bruno will have a table set up in the E.J. Thomas Hall lobby. If you have a clarinet languishing in your closet, this might be the time to find it a new home.

ELAINE **GUREGIAN**

The instruments don't have to be in perfect condition. The Taylor Band and Orchestra music store will repair them before passing them along.

Ohlsson, a repeat performer on the Tuesday Musical series, will play music of Prokofiev, Chopin, Justin Dello Joio and Rachmaninoff for his recital, which begins at 7:30 tonight. For tickets, call the E.J. Thomas Hall box office at 330-972-7570 or Tuesday Musical at 330-972-2342.

Above, clockwise from top: From the *Akron Beacon Journal,* May 6, 2008; Wynton Marsalis and Barbara Feld backstage, 2011; Marie Brooker, Tuesday Musical scholarship committee chair, 1998

Opposite, clockwise from top: From the *Akron Beacon Journal,* March 28, 2006; November 29, 2007 letter from Michele Monigold thanking Tuesday Musical for the student voucher program

Tuesday Musical Memories

"Tuesday Musical is an extraordinary organization, and I'm honored to have been presented as a young artist with my teacher, Josef Gingold, and later to have returned as an established artist. If only every arts organization could provide free tickets to youth!! I look forward to performing for them in the future."
—JOSHUA BELL

"In all of the forty-six years of my active membership in Tuesday Musical Association, this great organization has been one of the most important and happiest endeavors of my life in Akron, not only musically, but for the friendships that developed."
—MARIAN LOTT

"I admire and celebrate the spirit of the women who founded the association. In a time when the fine arts are struggling in our country, this organization's dedication to building and serving an eager audience with the best in musical performance and education is inspiring."
—RENÉE FLEMING

"I have fond memories of the concerts I've played for you in the past. I hope we can do it again in the future. All my best wishes."
—ITZHAK PERLMAN

"It's already impressive for any institution to have survived 125 years, but the way that the Tuesday Musical Association audience has grown and evolved with the times is truly a tribute to the enlightened leadership of Barbara Feld. Every time I have appeared under the association's auspices, I have enjoyed not only the enthusiasm of the public, but the attention and age spans of the audience. The devotion to celebrating the intersection between a great community and live performance is palpable."
—YO-YO MA

"[A]n absolutely incredible legacy and gift to the greater Akron area. [T]he Tuesday Musical audience demonstrates a highly adventurous spirit. We hope that tradition and curiosity together will help to ensure the next 125 years to come!"
—BROOKLYN RIDER

"My experience with the Tuesday Musical Association showed me that there is good reason for [their] unusual longevity; a staff that cares deeply about the audience, the artists, and the art, and a strong connection to the community. Congratulations to Barbara Feld and all who have worked so hard for something that has truly become an indispensable piece of the arts in Ohio."
—JOSHUA ROMAN

"We consider ourselves so very fortunate to have been members of Tuesday Musical while we lived in Akron. It is hard to describe what being members meant to us because our association with the organization was so thorough, wonderful, and at times life-changing. From luminary concerts by famed artists such as Marc-André Hamelin, Yo-Yo Ma, and Renée Fleming; to young emerging artists like the Sphinx Chamber Orchestra and the Imani Winds; to the annual Cleveland Orchestra appearance; and finally to having the joy and opportunity to personally perform on the members series, it has all been most fulfilling. Tuesday Musical executes its mission in a profound and exceptional manner."
—BONNIE AND JAMES ROSE, JR.

"Whether it was the Five Browns, Wynton Marsalis, or the Cleveland Orchestra, my music students have benefited immeasurably from the experiences that Tuesday Musical has given to our music department. Over the past seven years I have brought twenty to thirty students on average to every performance and have never been disappointed. My students have been equally enthralled and amazed by each performance. The variety of the concerts has been of great benefit as well. Please keep up the great work you do for music education in our state."
—DR. RANDOLPH LAYCOCK, CHAIRMAN, MUSIC DEPARTMENT, VALLEY FORGE HIGH SCHOOL, PARMA HEIGHTS

"Tuesday Musical Association has been a part of my life since I was very young. As a child, I remember attending classical concerts at E. J. Thomas Hall with my mother. A highlight of my college experience was winning a Tuesday Musical scholarship for piano in 1996, and now I'm a music technology teacher at McKinley High School in Canton. I have brought my students to concerts through the student ticket voucher program. It's a pretty awesome thing to watch as their minds and ears literally open to new musical sounds and textures. Tuesday Musical's gift is of extraordinary value, especially to those kids whose limited financial resources would otherwise prevent such an experience."
—**BRIAN LASKO**

"I was so excited that we had tickets to see and hear Yo-Yo Ma play. My dad talked to Mrs. Feld about me and how much I admired the artist, and she promised to try to get us invited to the reception for Mr. Ma. Not only did she get us in to the reception, she introduced me to him! Mr. Ma was warm, kind, and encouraging. I could not believe how humble, down to earth, and funny he was. We talked and laughed and I have some wonderful photographs of the two of us. One of them has been up on our mantle in a place of honor ever since. Whenever I look at it, it reminds me of that magical evening. It inspires me to practice too!"
—**MILES SLACK**

Appendix

Past Presidents of Tuesday Musical

Celia Ashmun Baker
(see bio, p. 96)

Lottie M. Merriman Houghton

Helen Storer Collins
(see bio, p. 97)

Harriet Day Parsons

Minnie Etta Riggs Heneberger
(see bio, p. 110)

Laura L. Day Andrews

Katherine Musser Bruot
(see bio, p. 107)

Jessie L. Wolfe Otis

Gertrude Penfield Seiberling
(honorary, see bio, p. 112)

Ada Armstrong House

Eva J. Proctor Heintselman

Ella Bigelow

G. Adeline Voss-Eichelberger

Clara B. Smith Collins

Effie D. Metcalf Bowman
(see bio, p. 120)

Winnifred Winn Guinther

Helen Ferryman Warford

Irene S. Crain

Jeanette C. Spaght Voth

Alice Palmer Hoak

Florence D. Eckert Dietz

Fama Noyes Keith

Helen Pepper Grant

Helen Drummond Christy

Helen K. Schmiedel Barnes

Anna M. Brock

Hariette Brooks Hunt

Estelle Fossee Ruth

Alice Memminger Stempel

Lydia Berthlesdorf Colopy

Ellen Mayl Herbreich

Isabelle Zehner Infield

Mary Ellen Gilpatric Nurmi

Mabel L. Lamborn Graham
(see bio, p. 133)

Carolyn Frye Ryan

Mary Helen Bowers

Marlene Murschel Unger

Jane White Kaufman

Ann Anthony Meck

Betty Jeffries Sloan

Billie Ream Whitum

Marcianne Herr

Dodi Sethman Meade

Jerry Davidson
(first male president)

Dorothy Lepp

Pat Sargent

Robert Fischer

Although every effort has been made to verify the past presidents of Tuesday Musical, in the very early years, chorus directors were probably in charge of operations. These chorus directors included Gustave Siegel, N. L. Glover, Anna Berry, Helen Storer Collins, Katherine Parsons, and Charles Clemens.